Simply Adorable Crochet

2 0 of the Cutest Projects Ever!

Simply Adorable Crochet

40 of the Cutest Projects Ever!

Maki Oomaci

Race Point
PUBLISHING

A division of Book Sales, Inc.
276 Fifth Avenue Suite 206
New York, New York 10001

RACE POINT PUBLISHING and the distinctive
Race Point Publishing logo are trademarks of Book Sales, Inc.

This 2013 edition published by Race Point Publishing by arrangement with The Book Shop, Ltd.

Based on the works *Amigurumi no Mori* and *Amigurumi no Chiisana Zakka* by Maki Oomaci,
first published in Japan by Gakken Publishing Co, Ltd, 2011.

TRANSLATOR Nikki Sato
CROCHET EDITOR Rebekah Phinney Greenwood
PROJECT EDITOR Sherry Gerstein
DESIGNER Tim Palin Creative

ISBN-13: 978-1-937994-12-9

Printed in China

2 4 6 8 10 9 7 5 3

www.racepointpub.com

Contents

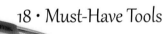

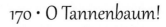
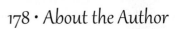

Introduction

Cute little critters, tasty treats, holiday decorations and more, this book includes a wide variety of crochet patterns to make and keep, or give away as gifts to friends and family. Step-by-step instructions include both diagrams and photographs.

Besides being simply adorable, the patterns in this book are fun to make. Beginning with standing animals that are worked flat, making it easy to count stitches, these projects are perfect for beginners as they build their crochet skills. More difficult techniques, like crocheting in the round and crocheting around a chain, are gradually introduced.

The small accessories are quick to make and are perfect for enclosing in a card or using as an embellishment on a perfectly wrapped gift.

Ready for Your First Project?

Before starting a project, read the instructions through carefully so you have a good idea of how to proceed. Then review the equipment list and assemble your tools and materials. You don't want to get caught mid-project without enough yarn or the right kind of hook.

What's It Called?

The word for cute crocheted animals and anthropomorphized toys is *amigurumi*. Knitted toys are called *mochi-mochi*. Both words are Japanese.

Stitches

⬭ Chain stitch (ch)

1 Turn the hook as shown.

2 Make a loop.

3 Yarn over and pull through the loop on hook.

4 Yarn over and pull through again.

5 Repeat step 4 to make the necessary length of chain.

✕ Single Crochet (sc)

When starting a row of single crochet, always begin with a turning chain of one stitch.

Turning chain, 1 stitch

1 Insert the hook from front to back into next stitch of starting chain. Yarn over hook and pull through the stitch to the front.

2 Yarn over hook again and pull through both loops on the hook.

3 Repeat first two steps for next stitch.

4 Continue until row is complete.

Half-Double Crochet (hdc)

When starting a row of half-double crochet, always start with a turning chain of two stitches.

Turning chain, 2 stitches
Skip first stitch or chain

1 Yarn over hook, then insert the hook from front to back into next stitch of starting chain. Yarn over hook and pull through the stitch to the front.

2 Yarn over hook again and pull through all three loops on the hook.

3 Repeat steps for remainder of row.

Having trouble keeping track of your rows? Try using a row counter. Just give it a click at the end of each row and it keeps the number of your current row right in front of you so you don't get lost.

Double Crochet (dc)

When starting a row of double crochet, always start with a turning chain of three stitches.

Turning chain, 3 stitches
Skip first stitch or chain

1 Yarn over hook, then insert the hook from front to back into next stitch of starting chain. Yarn over hook and pull through the stitch to the front.

2 Yarn over hook again and pull through first two loops on hook.

3 Yarn over again and pull through remaining two loops on hook.

4 Repeat steps for remainder of row.

Single Crochet Increase (sc inc)

Single crochet twice into same stitch.

 ## Single Crochet Decrease (sc2tog)

1 Draw a loop through first stitch (do NOT yarn over and complete stitch), then insert the hook into the second stitch and pull through. You will have three loops on the hook.

2 Yarn over and pull through all three loops.

 ## Double Crochet Increase (dc inc)

Double crochet twice into same stitch.

 ## Slip Stitch (sl st)

1 Insert the hook from front to back into next stitch and yarn over.

2 Draw yarn through both the chain and the loop on your hook.

Double Crochet Cluster (dc CL)

1 Yarn over, insert the hook into the next stitch, yarn over and pull loop through stitch. Yarn over again and draw the yarn through first two loops on hook.

2 Yarn over, insert the hook in the same stitch, yarn over and pull loop through, yarn over and pull through first two loops on hook. Repeat step 2 as many times as cluster indicates.

3 Yarn over again and pull through all loops on the hook.

4 Example shown is a 3 dc CL.

 # Popcorn Stitch (pc)

1 Make five double crochet stitches in next stitch. Pull loop on hook bigger than usual. Remove hook from loop. Reinsert hook into first double crochet stitch, and back through the working loop. Pull through as shown with arrow.

2 Make one chain stitch to pull entire stitch together.

 # Ridge Stitch or Through the Back Loop (tbl)

1 Insert hook from front to back in the back portion of the stitch only.

2 Yarn over, pull through and work as single crochet.

Crocheting in the Round

Begin by making a center ring:

Place a locking stitch marker in the first stitch of a new round to help you keep track.

1 Wrap the yarn twice around your index finger, creating a ring.

2 Insert hook through the center of the ring, yarn over and pull through.

3 Yarn over and pull through to make a chain stitch.

4 For next stitch, insert the hook into the ring, yarn over and pull through.

5 Yarn over and pull through as shown.

6 First single crochet of the round is now complete.

Pull tail

7 Repeat steps 4 and 5 to make the necessary number of stitches. Pull the tail of the yarn tight to close up the center ring.

8 To finish the round, make a slip stitch in the first stitch of previous round.

Tips and Techniques for Assembling a Figure

Here are the techniques you'll need to piece figures together, plus some of my favorite tips and tricks that I've learned over the years. Please note that a contrasting color yarn is used in these photos to help you see how to execute the steps. You will want to use a matching yarn when working on your own projects.

Joining Pieces Together

When joining body parts together, match the lettered star points to each other as indicated in the crochet charts and sew the pieces together using the whipstitch. (See pages 22–23 and 70–71 for step-by-step photos that focus on the techniques for assembling standing-style animals and crocheted-in-the-round figures, respectively.)

1 First match one side of the main body and the underbody together, and sew together using the whipstitch.

2 This is what the first whipstitch of the first row will look like.

3 Use one whipstitch per each row of piece.

Stuffing Your Animal

This is an important step; how you stuff your animal influences the shape of the body and the expression of its face. Different parts of the body require varying amounts of stuffing. Try not to break the stuffing up into small bits because it will make your figures look lumpy when stuffed.

1 Use a dense amount of stuffing for the head. This will ensure that it won't deform the shape of the head when you add face details.

2 Use the backside of a crochet hook to stuff animal legs to a medium density, providing a bit of firmness. Stuff evenly so that the legs are long and straight, so your animal can sit or stand properly.

3 Stuff the back of the animal last. Fill with enough stuffing so that it is full but still soft.

Fastening Yarn

To keep your crochet work from unraveling, you'll need to fasten it by tying the end of the yarn.

1 Pull up the final loop of the last stitch and pass the needle back through the loop you've created.

2 Pull the end of the yarn to tighten the knot.

Cutting the Yarn After Stuffing

After you've fastened the yarn, continue by passing the yarn through the body and the head to further ensure that your work does not unravel.

1 Using a tapestry needle, pass the yarn through the body at a hidden point. Return the needle through the body back to the fastening point.

2 Cut the yarn at the very edge of the body so tail of yarn is hidden inside.

How to Weave in Ends

Thread tail end of yarn into yarn needle, then pass it through the back of a few stitches to weave in, and cut the yarn. This will conceal the tails of your work, and will also ensure your project won't unravel.

Must-Have Tools

These are the basic tools you'll need on hand to make the projects:

Crochet Hook

The size of the crochet hook depends on the thickness of the yarn that will be used. Sizes range from 2.00 mm up to as large as 16.00 mm! The most commonly used hooks have a letter (B–Q) assigned to them. The bulkier the yarn, the bigger the hook you'll want to use, and vice versa.

Tapestry Needle

Use a tapestry needle to sew pieces together or add defining decorative details to a figure. You should match the eye of the needle to the thickness of the yarn being used.

Locking Stitch Marker

Stitch markers help to mark certain points in your work, such as the position of ears or other sewn-on pieces. They are also a convenient way to track the beginning of rows in the round.

Long Thread Needle

Use the longest thread needle you can find. You want something that is long enough to pass through the entire body of your crocheted figure so you can easily sew on eyes, tails, etc.

Marking/Blocking Pins

Some people like to use special marking pins for knitting to position and hold parts together while sewing up openings and attaching pieces to the main figure. Use a pin with a rounded point so it will not split your yarn.

Row Counter

This tool will help you keep count of your stitches and rows. Just push the top of the counter each time a stitch or row (whatever you are counting) is completed. And yes, there is even an app for that. If you have a smart phone, search your application marketplace for "stitch counting apps."

Scissors

You will need scissors to cut the yarn. I recommend using a pair of small, needle-nose scissors that will allow precise trimming without damaging your project.

Recommended Materials
Pick the right materials for your chosen project.

Basic Yarn

A basic yarn is usually made of acrylic or wool, frequently a blend of both. It is suitable for all skill levels, including beginners, because it has a consistent thickness, making it easy to count your stitches. It comes in a variety of colors and weights and can easily be found in most craft stores.

Specialty Yarns

There's a wide variety of specialty yarns available, such as mohair and variable-thickness yarns, especially in your local yarn store. While they may make it harder to count your stitches, specialty yarns allow you to achieve creative effects that regular yarns can't. If you are new to specialty yarns, I recommend that you practice crocheting with it before using it on a real project.

Cotton Thread

Use cotton thread when attaching buttons for eyes or detailing to your figures. Use it with a thread needle; tapestry needles can be too thick to pass through the holes in buttons. But if you find it too difficult to pass thick yarn through your thread needle, thread the needle with cotton thread and tie one end into a small loop. Then thread the yarn through the loop and pull the yarn through.

Toy Stuffing

Use toy stuffing to fill out your figures. I recommend using acrylic or polyester stuffing because it is light and easy to use.

Plastic Safety Eyes

There are special plastic eyes that are made specifically for stuffed toys like these. They have a stem that is inserted through the material and snapped into place with a plastic washer. The projects in this book use solid black eyes, but they come in a range of colors and styles. Use them to ensure that your finished project is child safe.

Finishing Touches

These materials will make your toys even cuter and more lifelike!

1. Transparent fishing line (also known as monofilament)—This is great for making whiskers on animals like the kittens on page 34.

2. Ribbon—A small piece of embroidered ribbon is the perfect finishing accessory for animals like the donkey on page 46. Or choose a small length of narrow grosgrain ribbon to add cute detailing to other animals.

Baby Animals

A Pair of Goats

FOCUS ON TECHNIQUE:
Making a Standing-Style Figure

How do you make a 3-D figure out of some yarn and a crochet hook? How do you take flat pieces of work and put them all together? These step-by-step instructions show you how.

The body, head, arms and legs are crocheted in one piece so the figure stands firm and stable. This pattern is broken up step by step to show you how these pieces take form, and then how they should come together. These steps can be used as reference for standing-style animals as well as for sitting figures.

Materials:

- Bulky-weight yarn (wool blend) in two colors (shown here: black and white), 60 yds (36g) each

- Medium-weight yarn (wool blend) in pink, small amount for mouth and nose details.

Tools:

- US Size H/8 (5.0mm) crochet hook

- Tapestry or yarn needle

- Toy stuffing, 30g each

- Two black buttons or safety animal eyes (9 mm)

- Embroidered ribbon, 14 ins. each (optional)

Measurements:

Finished size is 7 x 6 x 3 ins. (18 x 15.5 x 8 cm)

Note that measurements are approximate and will vary due to tension and yarn choice.

Pattern Notes:

This pattern is worked flat, back and forth in single crochet, creating four main body pieces and four detailing pieces. It is then assembled afterwards with yarn and a tapestry needle using the whipstitch.

Stitches Used:

Crochet: chain stitch (ch), turning chain (tch), single crochet (sc), single crochet increase (sc inc), single crochet decrease (sc dec), slip stitch (sl st). Piecing and details: whipstitch, embroidery. (See pages 10–13 for detailed stitch instructions)

1 **Begin with front leg:** ch 4. The three lower chain stitches are the "starting chain" and the one above is the "turning chain."

2 **Row 1:** Starting with the second chain from the hook, sc in each ch, 3 sc made. Ch 1. A ch 1 is at the end of every row. This is for the turning chain (tch), which is needed to begin the next row. The charts show this at the beginning of each row.

3 **Rows 2–10:** Repeat row 1. At end of row, keep loop on hook. Front leg is completed.

4 **Begin main body:** with loop remaining on hook, ch 14 (includes one for tch).

Row 1: Starting with the second chain from the hook, sc 16, ch 1. Be careful not to twist the chain when starting this row.

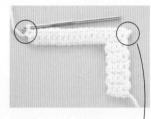

5 **Row 2:** sc inc, sc 15, sc inc, ch 1. 18 sts total.

Single crochet increase will look like this.

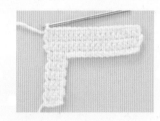

6 **Rows 3–5:** sc in each st across piece, ch 1.

7 **Row 6:** sc2tog, sc 14, sc2tog, ch 1.

8 **Row 7:** sc2tog, sc 14, keep loop on hook. Main body is complete.

9 **Begin head:** With loop remaining on hook, ch 6 (includes 1 for tch).

Row 1: Taking care not to twist the chain, start with second chain from the hook, sc 9, sc2tog, ch 1. Turn work here, before the end of body row.

10 **Rows 2–5:** sc 10, ch 1.

Row 6: sc 8, sc2tog, ch 1.

Row 7: sc2tog, sc 5, sc2tog, ch 1.

Row 8: sc 5, sc2tog, ch 1.

Row 9: sc2tog, sc 2, sc2tog.

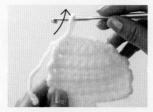

11 Cut the yarn, leaving a 6-in. tail, then pull yarn through. Head is complete.

12 **Begin hind leg as follows:** Reattach yarn at the bottom end of body, opposite of front leg, ch 1 for starting ch.

13 **Row 1:** sc 5, ch 1.

Row 2: repeat row 1.

14 **Row 3:** sc 3, sc2tog, ch 1.

Row 4: sc2tog, sc 2, ch 1.

Rows 5–9: sc 3, ch 1.

Row 10: sc 3, cut the yarn, leaving a 6-in. tail, then pull yarn through. Hind leg is complete.

15 To round out rump, reattach yarn at the top end of body, ch 1 for starting chain. Sc 4, then sl st in next stitch.

16 Cut the yarn, leaving a 6-in. tail, then pull yarn through.

17 Repeat entire sequence to make a second identical body piece. You may choose to weave in all tail ends of yarn here, or leave them to use for sewing pieces together later.

Underbody and Inner Legs:

18 Begin with ch 2 (one starting ch and one turning ch).

19 **Row 1:** Starting with the second chain from the hook, sc 1, ch 1.

Row 2: sc inc, then ch 1.

20 **Rows 3–7:** sc 2, ch 1.

Row 8: sc 1, sc inc, ch 1.

Rows 9–12: sc 3, ch 1.

Row 13: sc2tog, sc 1, ch 1.

Rows 14–17: sc 2, ch 1.

Row 18: sc2tog, ch 1.

Row 19: sc 1. Cut the yarn, leaving a 6-in. tail, then pull yarn through. Belly section is complete.

21 Begin inner legs. Reattach yarn at the fourth row of belly for first hind leg.

Row 1: Ch 1, then sc 3 across side.

22 At the end of row 10, cut the yarn, leaving an 8-in. tail, then pull yarn through.

Repeat these rows on opposite side of belly for second hind leg.

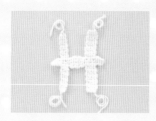

Back of Head:

23 For front inner legs, reattach yarn at row 15 of belly.

Row 1: ch 1, then sc 2 across side.

Rows 2–10: sc 2, then ch 1. At the end of row 10, cut the yarn, leaving an 8-in. tail, then pull yarn through. Repeat these rows on opposite side of belly for second front leg. Underbody and inner legs are complete.

24 As in underbody, begin with ch 2 (one starting ch and one turning ch).

Row 1: Starting with the second chain from the hook, sc 1, ch 1.

Row 2: sc inc, then ch 1.

Row 3: sc 1, sc inc, ch 1.

Row 4: sc 1, sc inc, sc 1, ch 1.

Row 5: sc 1, sc inc, sc 2, ch 1.

Rows 6–8: sc 5, ch 1.

Row 9: sc2tog, sc 1, sc2tog, cut the yarn, leaving an 8-in. tail, then pull yarn through. Back of head is complete.

Muzzle

25 Create the muzzle using the crochet-in-the-round method (see page 14 for detailed instructions). Begin by making a central ring. Ch 1 and sc 1 inside the loop as you would through a regular crochet stitch.

26 **Round 1:** sc 4 more stitches around the loop.

27 Pull the tail end of the yarn to tighten the center ring. Complete round 1 by making a sl st in the first sc of row. (Slip stitch at the end of each following round is worked the same way.)

Ears (make two):

Tail:

28 **Round 2:** ch 1, (sc 1, sc inc) twice, sc 1, sl st.

Round 3: ch 1, (sc inc, sc 1) three times, sc inc, sl st.

Round 4: ch 1, sc 11, sl st. Cut the yarn, leaving an 8-in. tail, then pull yarn through. Muzzle is complete.

29 Begin with ch 2.

Row 1: Starting with the second chain from the hook, sc 1, ch 1.

Row 2: sc inc, then ch 1.

Row 3: sc 1, sc inc, ch 1.

Row 4: sc 1, sc inc, sc 1, ch 1.

Row 5: sc 1, sc dec over next 2 sts, sc 1, ch 1 for tch.

Row 6: sc dec over next 2 sts, sc 1, ch 1 for tch.

Row 7: sc dec over 2 sts. Cut the yarn, leaving an 8-in. tail, then pull yarn through. Repeat for second ear.

30 **Row 1:** Being careful not to twist the chain, sc 7. Cut the yarn, leaving an 8-in. tail, then pull yarn through. Carefully fold the piece in half lengthwise and use the whipstitch (see page 16) to sew up the sides of the tail to create a tube.

Sew the Pieces Together:

See page 32 for more details on how to assemble standing-style animals.

31 Match the edge of the underbody to one of the main body pieces at the star points marked on the charts, and sew together with the whipstitch. You will work from the front of the figure to the back.

32 Sew second main body piece to the other side of underbody in a similar fashion, working back to front.

33 Now sew up around the head from front to back, matching star points. Leave the back open for stuffing. If using safety animal eyes, affix them now, before stuffing (follow package directions).

Stuffing:

43 Fill head, legs and body with toy stuffing.

44 Close up the back of the figure with whipstitch.

Attach the Muzzle, Tail, and Ears:

45 Pack the muzzle with a small amount of toy stuffing to give it shape. Place filled muzzle on face (use marking pins to hold placement if desired) and attach to face with tail end of yarn. Weave in end.

47 Use remaining tail ends of yarn and tapestry needle to close the bottom of the feet. Pull yarn tight to close up hole. Fasten off and weave in ends.

48 Using tail end of yarn, attach the tail to body.

49 Attach both ears (refer to crochet chart for placement).

51 If using buttons for eyes, attach them now (refer to crochet chart for placement). With small amount of pink yarn, add nose and mouth details with simple straight stitches. Tie ribbon around neck for embellishment, if desired.

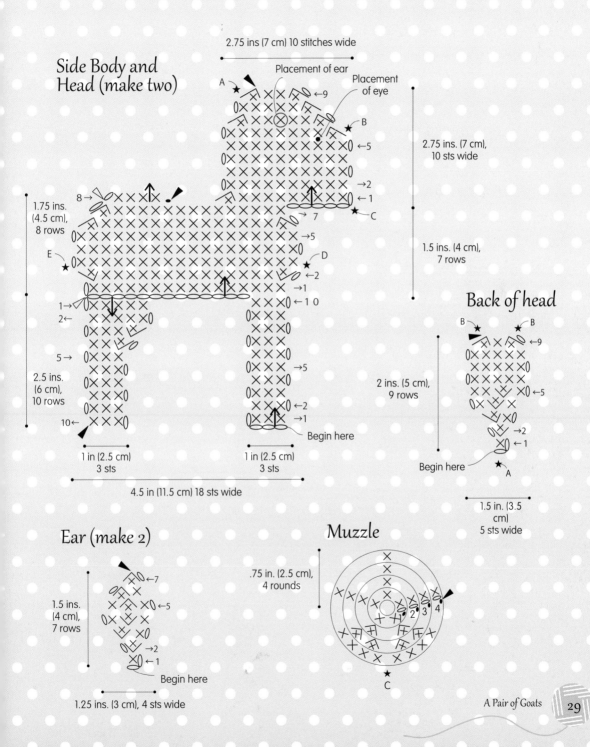

Side Body and Head (make two)

2.75 ins (7 cm) 10 stitches wide

Placement of ear

Placement of eye

A

B

←9

←5

→2
←1

→7

C

2.75 ins. (7 cm),
10 sts wide

1.5 ins. (4 cm),
7 rows

→5

D

←2
→1

←1 0

8→

1.75 ins.
(4.5 cm),
8 rows

E

1→
2←

5→

2.5 ins.
(6 cm),
10 rows

10←

→5

←2
→1

Begin here

1 in (2.5 cm)
3 sts

1 in (2.5 cm)
3 sts

4.5 in (11.5 cm) 18 sts wide

Back of head

B

B

←9

←5

→2
←1

2 ins. (5 cm),
9 rows

Begin here

A

1.5 in. (3.5 cm)
5 sts wide

Ear (make 2)

←7

←5

→2
←1

1.5 ins.
(4 cm),
7 rows

Begin here

1.25 ins. (3 cm), 4 sts wide

Muzzle

.75 in. (2.5 cm),
4 rounds

2 3 4

C

Underbody and Inner Legs

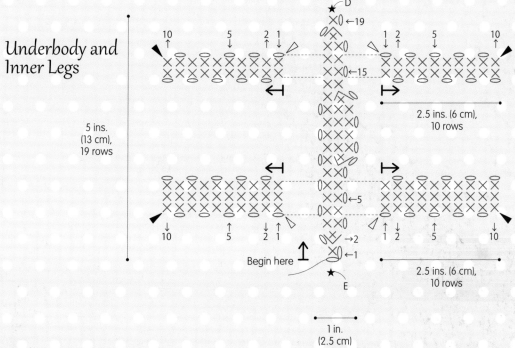

5 ins.
(13 cm),
19 rows

D

×0 ←19

×0 ←15

10
5
2 1

1 2
5
10

2.5 ins. (6 cm),
10 rows

←5

10
5
2 1

1 2
5
10

2.5 ins. (6 cm),
10 rows

Begin here

→2

←1

E

1 in.
(2.5 cm)
3 sts wide

Tail

.25 in.
(.5 cm)
1 row

×××××× ←1

Begin here

1.75 ins. (4.5
cm), 7 sts wide

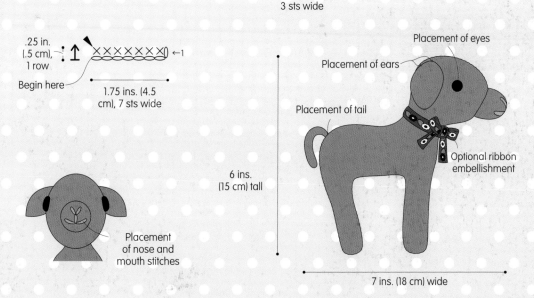

Placement of eyes

Placement of ears

Placement of tail

Optional ribbon
embellishment

6 ins.
(15 cm) tall

Placement
of nose and
mouth stitches

7 ins. (18 cm) wide

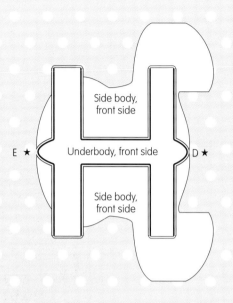

Side body, front side

Underbody, front side

E ★

D ★

Side body, front side

How to Assemble Body Parts—Standing-Style Animals

Goat, Kitten, Deer, Donkey, and Lamb

1. Starting at the D star points, place the two main body halves and the underbody pieces together as shown in the diagram. Using the whipstitch, sew the pieces together on one side to the E star points. (Use the bold line on the diagram for reference.) Leave the bottoms of the feet open. Then work your way back to the D starting point on the other side.

2. Once returning to the D star point, work your way up to C, again using the bold line for reference.

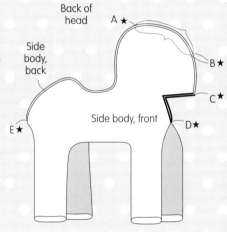

Back of head

A ★

Side body, back

B ★

C ★

Side body, front

E ★

D ★

3. Place the back of head piece to the main body piece. Match up the A star points and the B star points on the corresponding pieces. Sew up one side from B to A, then return down the other side back to B. (*Note: Sew C to B when making kittens; for all other animals, leave B to C open for muzzle in step 7.*)

4. Reattach a new piece of yarn at A (or use a tail end if you have left one) and begin sewing up the back of the head and down the neck. If you are using safety animal eyes, you will want to place them now. Stuff the legs, head and body with toy stuffing.

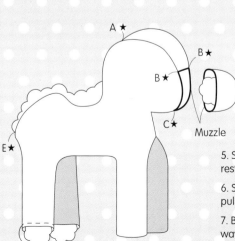

A ★

B ★

B ★

C ★

Muzzle

E ★

5. Stuff the back, while adjusting the shape to desired form, and sew up the rest of the body from A to E.

6. Sew up the bottoms of the feet with the remaining tail ends of yarn and pull tight.

7. Begin to attach the muzzle to the front the head. When you're about half way, fill it with toy stuffing to give it shape. Finish sewing around, secure yarn and weave in tail end.

Three Little Kittens

Materials:

- Bulky-weight yarn (acrylic and wool blend) in three different colors (shown here: dark gray, white, and mustard), 60 yds (36g) each.
- Medium-weight yarn (acrylic and wool blend) in brown or black, small amount for detailing.

Tools:

- US size H/8 (5.0mm) crochet hook
- Tapestry or yarn needle
- Sewing needle and cotton thread (if using buttons for eyes)
- Toy stuffing, 30g
- Two black buttons or safety animal eyes
- 9 ins. monofilament or fishing line for whisker embellishment, cut into three equal pieces.

Measurements:

Finished piece is 5.5 x 5.5 x 3 ins. (14 x 14 x 7.75 cm)

Note that measurements are approximate and will vary due to tension and yarn choice.

Pattern Notes:

This pattern is worked flat, back and forth in single crochet, creating three main body pieces and four detailing pieces. It is then assembled afterwards with yarn and a tapestry needle using the whipstitch. Monofilament is used to achieve whimsical whiskers.

Stitches Used:

Crochet: chain stitch (ch), turning chain (tch), single crochet (sc), single crochet increase (sc inc), single crochet decrease (sc2tog), slip stitch (sl st). Piecing and details: whipstitch, and embroidery. (See pages 10–13 for detailed instructions.)

Note: a ch 1 is at the end of every row. This is for the turning chain (tch), which is needed to begin the next row. The chart shows this at the beginning of each row.

Underbody and Inner Legs:

Begin with ch 2 (one starting ch and one turning ch).

Row 1: Starting with the second chain from the hook, sc 1, ch 1.

Row 2: sc inc, ch 1.

Rows 3–4: sc 2, ch 1.

Row 5: sc inc, sc 1, ch 1.

Rows 6–12: sc 3, ch 1.

Row 13: sc2tog, sc 1, ch 1.

Rows 14–17: sc 2, ch 1.

Row 18: sc2tog, ch 1.

Row 19: sc 1. Cut the yarn, leaving a 6-in. tail, then pull yarn through. Belly section is complete.

Begin inner legs. Reattach yarn at the fourth row of belly for first hind leg.

Row 1: Ch 1, then sc 3 across side.

Rows 2–8: sc 3, ch 1.

At the end of row 8, cut the yarn leaving an 8-in. tail, then pull yarn through.

Repeat these rows on opposite side of belly for second hind leg.

For front inner legs, reattach yarn at row 15 of belly.

Row 1: ch 1, then sc 2 across side.

Rows 2–8: sc 2, ch 1. At the end of row 10, cut the yarn leaving an 8-in. tail, then pull yarn through. Repeat these rows on opposite side of belly for second front leg. Underbody and inner legs are complete.

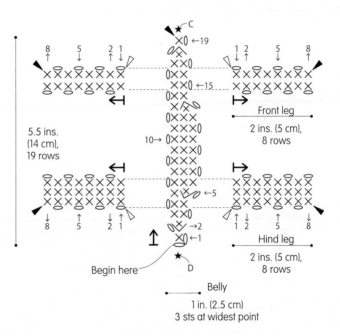

Head side

5.5 ins. (14 cm), 19 rows

Front leg
2 ins. (5 cm), 8 rows

Hind leg
2 ins. (5 cm), 8 rows

Begin here

Belly
1 in. (2.5 cm)
3 sts at widest point

Main Body, Head, Front and Hind Legs (make two):

Begin with front leg: ch 3.

Row 1: Starting with the second chain from the hook, sc in each ch, 2 sc made. Ch 1 for tch.

Row 2–8: sc 2. At end of row 8, keep loop on hook. Front leg is completed.

Begin main body: With loop remaining on hook, ch 13 (includes one for tch).

Row 1: Starting with the second chain from the hook, sc 14, ch 1. Be careful not to twist the chain when starting this row.

Row 2: sc inc, sc 12, sc inc, ch 1.

Row 3: sc 16, ch 1.

Row 4: sc2tog, sc 12, sc2tog, ch 1.

Row 5: sc2tog, sc 11, sc inc, ch 1. Continue working on this piece for head.

Begin head:

Row 1: sc inc, sc 3, sc inc, ch 1. Turn work without going all the way across piece.

Row 2: sc inc, sc 5, sc inc, ch 1.

Row 3: (sc inc) twice, sc 7, ch 1.

Row 4: sc 7, (sc2tog) twice, ch 1.

Row 5: sc2tog, sc 7, ch 1.

Row 6: sc 8, ch 1.

Row 7: sc 6, sc2tog, ch 1.

Row 8: sc2tog, sc 3, sc2tog. Cut the yarn leaving a 6-in. tail, then pull yarn through.

Begin hind leg as follows:
Reattach yarn at the bottom end of body, opposite of front leg, ch 1 for starting ch.

Row 1: work sc in next 4 sts, ch 1.

Row 2: sc2tog, sc 2, ch 1.

Row 3: sc 1, sc2tog, ch 1.

Rows 4–8: sc 2, ch 1. At end of row 8, cut the yarn leaving a 6-in. tail, then pull yarn through.

To round out rump, reattach yarn at the top end of body, ch 1 for starting chain.

Row 1: sc 4, then sl st in next stitch. Cut the yarn leaving a 6-in. tail, then pull yarn through. Main body piece is complete.

Note: you may choose to weave in ends at the end of each piece (see page 17 for how to weave in ends) or you can tuck them in as you stitch the pieces together.

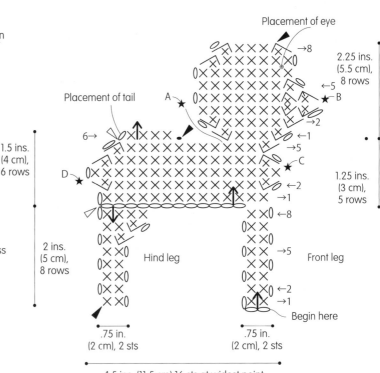

Placement of eye

2.25 ins. (5.5 cm), 8 rows

Placement of tail

1.25 ins. (3 cm), 5 rows

1.5 ins. (4 cm), 6 rows

Hind leg

Front leg

2 ins. (5 cm), 8 rows

Begin here

.75 in. (2 cm), 2 sts

.75 in. (2 cm), 2 sts

4.5 ins. (11.5 cm), 16 sts at widest point

◀ start new yarn
◁ break yarn

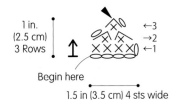

1 in.
(2.5 cm)
3 Rows

Begin here

1.5 in (3.5 cm) 4 sts wide

Ears (make two):

Begin with ch 5 (includes one for tch).

Row 1: sc 4, ch 1.

Row 2: (sc2tog) twice, ch 1.

Row 3: sc2tog, cut the yarn, leaving a 6-in. tail, then pull yarn through.

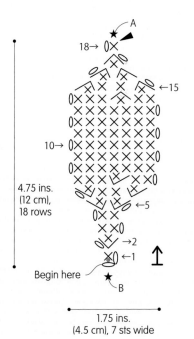

A

18→

←15

10→

4.75 ins.
(12 cm),
18 rows

←5

→2
←1

Begin here

B

1.75 ins.
(4.5 cm), 7 sts wide

Back of Head:

Begin with ch 2 (one starting ch and one turning ch).

Row 1: Starting with the second chain from the hook, sc 1, ch 1.

Row 2: sc inc, ch 1.

Rows 3 & 4: sc 2, ch 1.

Row 5: (sc inc) twice, ch 1.

Row 6: sc inc, sc 2, sc inc, ch 1.

Row 7: sc 2, sc inc, sc 3, ch 1.

Rows 8–13: sc 7, ch 1.

Row 14: sc 3, sc2tog, sc 2, ch 1.

Row 15: sc2tog, sc 2, sc2tog, ch 1.

Row 16: (sc2tog) twice, ch 1.

Row 17: sc2tog, ch 1.

Row 18: sc 1, cut the yarn, leaving an 8-in. tail, then pull yarn through.
Back of head is complete.

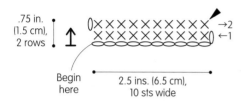

.75 in.
(1.5 cm),
2 rows

→2
←1

Begin
here

2.5 ins. (6.5 cm),
10 sts wide

←1

Begin here

Tail:

Begin with ch 11 (includes one for tch).

Rows 1–2: sc 10, ch 1. At the end of row 10, cut the yarn, leaving an 8-in. tail, then pull yarn through.

To close up tail, fold in half lengthwise and use the whipstitch to sew closed.

Nose Tip:

Make the nose tip using brown yarn, ch 2.

Row 1: In the second chain from the hook, sc inc, cut the yarn leaving an 8-in. tail, then pull yarn through.

Face Details:

Using the brown yarn and tapestry needle, whipstitch the nose tip to the center of the face. Embroider two straight stitches to create the mouth.

Glue the monofilament pieces in place, or loop them through behind the nose tip. Trim to desired length.

Sew the Pieces Together:

Use the instructions on page 32 for how to assemble standing-style animals. Use the charts throughout the pattern for reference and piece placement.

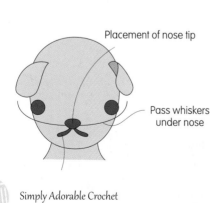

Placement of nose tip

Pass whiskers
under nose

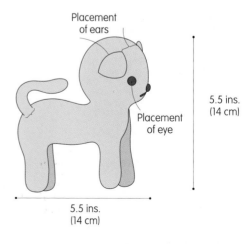

Placement
of ears

5.5 ins.
(14 cm)

Placement
of eye

5.5 ins.
(14 cm)

Deer

Materials:

- Bulky-weight yarn (acrylic and wool blend) in light brown, 60 yds (36g)
- Bulky-weight yarn (acrylic and wool blend) in white, 8 yds (10g)
- Bulky-weight yarn (acrylic and wool blend) in black, 1 yd (1g)
- Medium-weight yarn (acrylic and wool blend) in white, 10 yds (5g)

Tools:

- US size E/4 (3.5mm) crochet hook
- US size H/8 (5.0mm) crochet hook
- Tapestry or yarn needle
- Sewing needle and cotton thread (if using buttons for eyes)
- Toy stuffing, 30g
- Two black buttons or safety animal eyes

Stitches Used:

Crochet: chain stitch (ch), turning chain (tch), single crochet (sc), single crochet increase (sc inc), single crochet decrease (sc2tog), slip stitch (sl st). Piecing and details: whipstitch, and embroidery. (See pages 10–13 for detailed crochet instructions.)

Note: a ch 1 is at the end of every row. This is for the turning chain (tch), which is needed to begin the next row. The chart shows this at the beginning of each row.

Measurements:

Finished piece is 7.75 x 7 x 3 ins. (19.5 x 18 x 7.5 cm)

Note that measurements are approximate and will vary due to tension and yarn choice.

Pattern Notes:

This pattern is worked flat, back and forth in single crochet, creating four main body pieces and seven detailing pieces. It is then assembled afterwards with yarn and a tapestry needle using the whipstitch.

Learn how to make this little cluster of nuts on pages 54–55.

Underbody and Inner Legs:

Using the US size H/8 crochet hook and bulky-weight white yarn, begin with ch 2 (one starting ch and one tch).

Row 1: Starting with the second chain from the hook, sc 1, ch 1.

Row 2: sc inc, ch 1.

Rows 3–7: sc 2, ch 1.

Row 8: sc 1, sc inc, ch 1.

Rows 9–12: sc 3, ch 1.

Row 13: sc2tog, sc 1, ch 1.

Rows 14–17: sc 2, ch 1.

Row 18: sc2tog, ch 1.

Row 19: sc 1. Cut the yarn, leaving a 6-in. tail, then pull yarn through. Belly section is complete.

Begin inner legs. Reattach yarn at the fourth row of belly for first hind leg.

Row 1: ch 1, sc 3 across side, ch 1.

Rows 2–12: sc 3, ch 1.

At the end of row 10, cut the yarn, leaving an 8-in. tail, then pull yarn through.

Repeat these rows on opposite side of belly for second hind leg.

For front inner legs, reattach yarn at row 15 of belly.

Row 1: ch 1, sc 2 across side.

Rows 2–12: sc 2 the ch 1. At the end of row 10, cut the yarn, leaving an 8-in. tail, then pull yarn through. Repeat these rows on opposite side of belly for second front leg. Underbody and inner legs are complete.

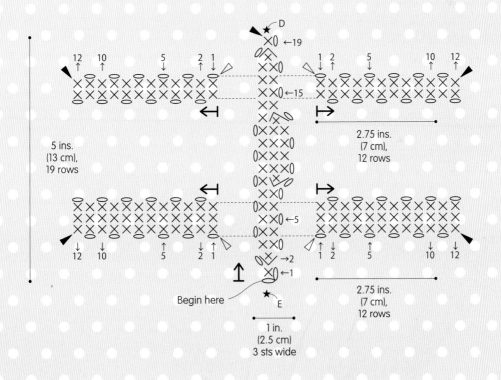

Main Body, Head, Front and Hind Legs (make two):

Using size H/8 crochet hook and light brown yarn, begin with front leg: ch 4.

Row 1: Starting with the second chain from the hook, sc in each ch, 3 sc made. Ch 1.

Row 2: sc 3, ch 1.

Rows 3–12: Repeat row 2. At end of row 12, keep loop on hook. Front leg is completed.

Begin main body: With loop remaining on hook, ch 14 (includes one for tch).

Row 1: Starting with the second chain from the hook, sc 16, ch 1. Be careful not to twist the chain when starting this row.

Row 2: sc 15, sc inc, ch 1.

Rows 3–5: sc 16, ch 1.

Row 6: sc inc, sc 16, ch 1.

Row 7: sc2tog, sc 16, ch 1.

Row 8: sc 5. Ch 1. Turn work without going all the way across piece.

Row 9: sc 3, sc2tog, ch 1.

Row 10: sc 4, ch 1.

Row 11: sc 4. At end of row, keep loop on hook.

Begin head: With loop remaining on hook, ch 5 (includes one for tch).

Row 1: sc 7, sc inc, ch 1.

Row 2: sc inc, sc 8, ch 1.

Rows 3–5: sc 10, ch 1.

Row 6: sc 8, sc2tog, ch 1.

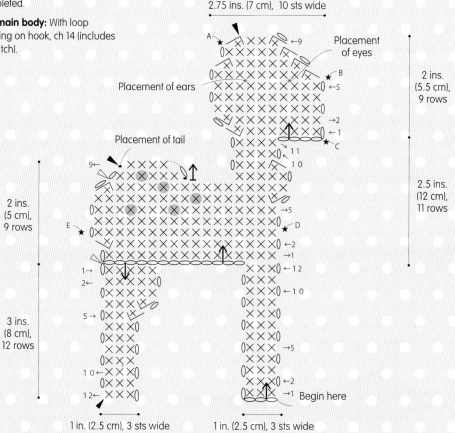

2.75 ins. (7 cm), 10 sts wide

Placement of eyes

Placement of ears

Placement of tail

2 ins. (5.5 cm), 9 rows

2.5 ins. (12 cm), 11 rows

2 ins. (5 cm), 9 rows

3 ins. (8 cm), 12 rows

1 in. (2.5 cm), 3 sts wide

1 in. (2.5 cm), 3 sts wide

4.5 ins. (11.5 cm)

Begin here

Row 7: sc2tog, sc 5, sc2tog, ch 1.

Row 8: sc 5, sc2tog, ch 1.

Row 9: sc2tog, sc 2, sc2tog. Cut the yarn, leaving a 6-in. tail, then pull yarn through.

Begin hind leg as follows: Reattach yarn at the bottom end of body, opposite of front leg, ch 1 for starting ch.

Row 1: work sc in next 5 sts, ch 1.

Rows 2–3: repeat row 1.

Row 4: sc2tog, sc 3, ch 1.

Row 5: sc 2, sc2tog, ch 1.

Row 6–12: sc 3, ch 1. At end of row 12, cut the yarn, leaving a 6-in. tail, then pull yarn through.

To round out rump, reattach yarn at the top end of body, ch1 for starting chain.

Row 1: sc 6, then sl st in next stitch, ch 1.

Row 2: Skip first stitch then sc 4, then sl st in next stitch. Cut the yarn, leaving a 6-in. tail, then pull yarn through.

Outer Ears (make two):

Using the US size H/8 crochet hook and light brown yarn, begin with ch 2.

Row 1: Starting with the second chain from the hook, sc 1, ch 1.

Row 2: sc inc, ch 1.

Row 3: (sc inc) twice, ch 1.

Row 4: sc inc, sc 2, sc inc , ch 1.

Rows 5–6: sc 6, ch 1.

Row 7: sc2tog, sc 2, sc2tog, ch 1.

Row 8: sc 4, ch 1.

Row 9: (sc2tog) twice. Cut the yarn, leaving an 8-in. tail, then pull yarn through.

Inner Ears (make two):

Using the US size E/4 crochet hook, with medium weight white yarn, ch 4.

Row 1: Starting with the second chain from the hook, sc 3, ch 1.

Row 2: sc inc, sc 2, ch 1.

Row 3: sc inc, sc 3, ch 1.

Row 4: sc inc, sc 4, ch 1.

Row 5: sc inc, sc 5, ch 1.

Row 6: sc inc, sc 6, ch 1.

Rows 7–8: sc 8, ch 1.

Row 9: sc2tog, sc 6, ch 1.

Row 10: sc2tog, sc 5, ch 1.

Row 11: sc2tog, sc 4, ch 1.

Row 12: sc2tog, sc 3, ch 1.

Row 13: sc2tog twice, ch 1.

Row 14: sc2tog, cut the yarn, leaving a 6-in. tail, then pull yarn through.

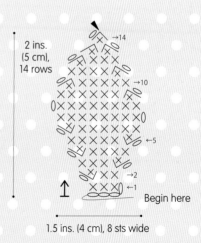

2 ins. (5 cm), 14 rows

1.5 ins. (4 cm), 8 sts wide

Begin here

2.25 ins. (5.5 cm), 9 Rows

Begin here

1.5 ins. (4 cm), 6 sts wide

Muzzle:

Using the US size H/8 crochet hook with the bulky-weight white yarn, begin with the crochet-in-the-round method by making a central ring. (See page 14 for detailed instructions.)

Round 1: sc 5 stitches around the loop. Pull the tail end of the yarn to tighten the center ring. Complete round 1 by making a sl st in the first sc of row.

Round 2: ch 1, (sc 1, sc inc) twice, sc 1. Sl st into first stitch of round.

Round 3: ch 1, (sc inc, sc 1) three times, sc inc. Sl st into first stitch of round.

Round 4: ch 1, sc 11, sl st into first stitch of round. Cut the yarn, leaving an 8-in. tail, then pull yarn through. Muzzle is complete.

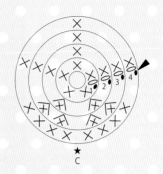

Back of Head:

Using the US size H/8 crochet hook and light brown yarn, begin with ch 2 (one starting ch and one tch).

Row 1: Starting with the second chain from the hook, sc 1, ch 1.

Row 2: sc inc, ch 1.

Row 3: sc 1, sc inc, ch 1.

Row 4: sc 1, sc inc, sc1, ch 1.

Row 5: sc 1, sc inc, sc 2, ch 1.

Rows 6–8: sc 5, ch 1.

Row 9: sc2tog, sc 1, sc2tog, cut the yarn, leaving an 8-in. tail, then pull yarn through. Back of head is complete.

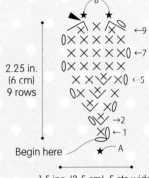

2.25 in. (6 cm) 9 rows

Begin here

1.5 ins. (3.5 cm), 5 sts wide

Tail:

Using the US size H/8 crochet hook and light brown yarn, begin with ch 5 (includes one for tch).

Row 1–2: sc 4, ch 1.

At the end of row 2, cut the yarn, leaving an 8-in. tail, then pull yarn through.

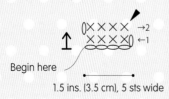

Begin here

1.5 ins. (3.5 cm), 5 sts wide

Tip of Nose:

Using the US size H/8 crochet hook and the black yarn, ch 2.

Row 1: sc 1 into second ch from hook, cut the yarn, leaving an 8-in. tail, then pull yarn through. Tip of nose is complete.

Begin here

Embroider the Spots

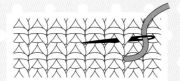

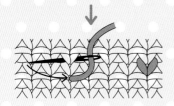

To make the spots, use the tapestry needle and medium-weight white yarn. Refer to the main body crochet chart for proper placement. Pass needle from front to back, through one stitch, pass the needle to the front and pass the needle back through where you started. Make V-shape. Pass the needle through to next spot position and repeat.

Sew the Pieces Together:

Use the instructions on page 32 for how to assemble standing-style animals. Use the charts throughout the pattern for reference and piece placement.

Use the whipstitch to attach the tip of nose to the muzzle, and the inner ears to outer ears. When attaching ears, fold them in half slightly at the base to give them shape.

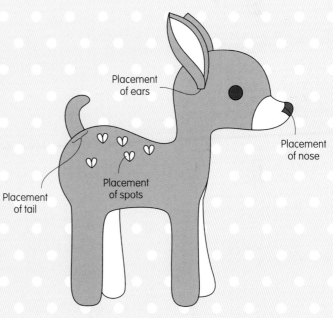

Placement of ears

Placement of nose

Placement of tail

Placement of spots

Donkey

Materials:

- Bulky-weight yarn (acrylic and wool blend) in gray, 60 yds (36g)
- Bulky-weight yarn (acrylic and wool blend) in white, 8 yds (15g)
- Bulky-weight yarn (acrylic and wool blend) in black, 1 yd (3g)
- Medium-weight yarn in black, small amount for nose details

Tools:

- US size H/8 (5.0mm) crochet hook
- Tapestry or yarn needle
- Sewing needle and cotton thread (if using buttons for eyes)
- Toy stuffing, 30g
- Two black buttons or safety animal eyes
- Embroidered tapestry ribbon for embellishment

Stitches Used:

Crochet: chain stitch (ch), turning chain (tch), single crochet (sc), single crochet increase (sc inc), single crochet decrease (sc2tog), slip stitch (sl st). Piecing and details: whipstitch, and embroidery. (See pages 10–13 for detailed instructions.)

*Note: a ch 1 is at the end of every row. This is for the turning chain (tch), which is needed to begin the next row. The chart shows this at the beginning of each row.

Measurements:

Finished piece is 7.5 x 7 x 3 ins. (19.5 x 18 x 7.5 cm)

*Note that measurements are approximate and will vary due to tension and yarn choice.

Pattern Notes:

This pattern is worked flat, back and forth in single crochet, creating four main body pieces and three detailing pieces. It is then assembled afterwards with yarn and a tapestry needle, using the whipstitch. Embellishment may be added at the end, if desired.

Underbody and Inner Legs:

Using the white yarn, begin with ch 2 (one starting ch and one turning ch).

Row 1: Starting with the second chain from the hook, sc 1, ch 1.

Row 2: sc inc, ch 1.

Rows 3–7: sc 2, ch 1.

Row 8: sc 1, sc inc, ch 1.

Rows 9–12: sc 3, ch 1.

Row 13: sc2tog, sc 1, ch 1.

Rows 14–18: sc 2, ch 1.

Row 19: sc2tog, ch 1.

Row 20: sc 1. Cut the yarn, leaving a 6-in. tail, then pull yarn through. Belly section is complete.

Begin inner legs. Reattach yarn at the fourth row of belly for first hind leg.

Row 1: Ch 1, sc 4 across side, ch 1.

Rows 2: sc 4, ch 1.

Row 3: sc 2, sc2tog, ch 1.

Rows 4–8: sc 3, ch 1. At end of row 8, cut the yarn leaving a 6-in. tail, leave loop on hook.

Row 9: Change to black yarn, ch 1 (acts as tch from previous row) sc 3, ch 1.

Row 10: sc 3. At the end of row 10, cut the yarn, leaving an 8-in. tail, then pull yarn through.

Repeat these rows on opposite side of belly for second hind leg.

For front inner legs, reattach yarn at row 15 of belly.

Row 1: ch 1, sc 3 across side.

Rows 2–8: sc 3, ch 1. At end of row 8, cut the yarn leaving a 6-in. tail, leave loop on hook.

Row 9: Change to black yarn, ch 1 (acts as tch from previous row) sc 3, ch 1.

Row 10: sc 3. At the end of row 10, cut the yarn, leaving an 8-in. tail, then pull yarn through.

Repeat these rows on opposite side of belly for second front leg. Underbody and inner legs are complete.

X = White yarn
Ⓧ = Black yarn

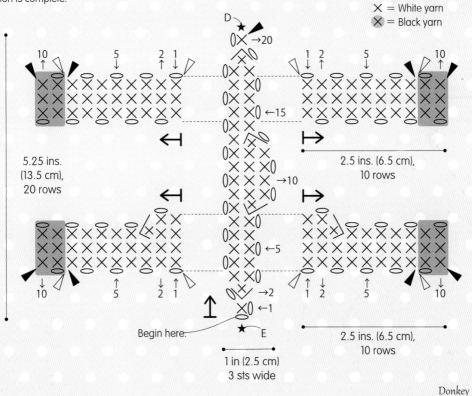

5.25 ins. (13.5 cm), 20 rows

2.5 ins. (6.5 cm), 10 rows

2.5 ins. (6.5 cm), 10 rows

Begin here.

1 in (2.5 cm)
3 sts wide

Main Body:

Using black yarn, begin with front leg: ch 5.

Starting with the second chain from the hook, sc in each ch, 4 sc made. Ch 1.

Row 2: sc 4, cut yarn, leaving loop on hook.

Row 3: Attach gray yarn, ch 1 (acts as tch from previous row) sc 4, ch 1.

Rows 4-10: sc 4, ch 1. At end of row 10, keep loop on hook. Front leg is complete.

Begin main body: With loop remaining on hook, ch 14 (includes one for tch).

Row 1: Starting with the second chain from the hook, sc 17, ch 1. Be careful not to twist the chain when starting this row.

Row 2: sc inc, sc 15, sc inc, ch 1.

Row 3: sc 19, ch 1.

Row 4: sc inc, sc 17, sc inc, ch 1.

Row 5: sc 21, ch 1.

Row 6: sc inc, sc 20, ch 1.

Row 7: sc 22, ch 1.

Row 8: sc inc, sc 19, sc2tog, ch 1.

Row 9: sc2tog, sc 20. At end of row, keep loop on hook.

Begin head: With loop remaining on hook, ch 6 (includes one for tch).

Row 1: sc 12, sc2tog, ch 1.

Row 2: sc 13, ch 1.

Row 3: sc 11, sc2tog, ch 1.

Row 4: sc 12, ch 1.

Row 5: sc2tog, sc 8, sc2tog, ch 1.

Row 6: sc 8, sc2tog, ch 1.

Row 7: sc2tog, sc 7, ch 1.

Row 8: sc2tog, sc 4, sc2tog. Cut the yarn, leaving a 6-in. tail, then pull yarn through.

Begin hind leg as follows: Reattach gray yarn at the bottom end of body, opposite of the front leg, ch 1 for starting ch.

Row 1: work sc in next 6 sts, ch 1.

Row 2: repeat row 1.

Row 3: sc 4, sc2tog, ch 1.

Row 4: sc2tog, sc 3, ch 1.

Rows 5–8: sc 4, ch 1. At end of row 8, cut the yarn leaving a 6-in. tail; leave loop on hook.

Row 9: Change to black yarn, ch 1 (acts as tch from previous row) sc 4, ch 1.

Row 10: sc 4, cut the yarn, leaving a 6-in. tail, then pull yarn through.

To round out rump, reattach yarn at the top end of body, ch1 for starting chain.

Row 1: sc 5, then sl st in next stitch. Cut the yarn, leaving a 6-in. tail, then pull yarn through. Main body piece is complete.

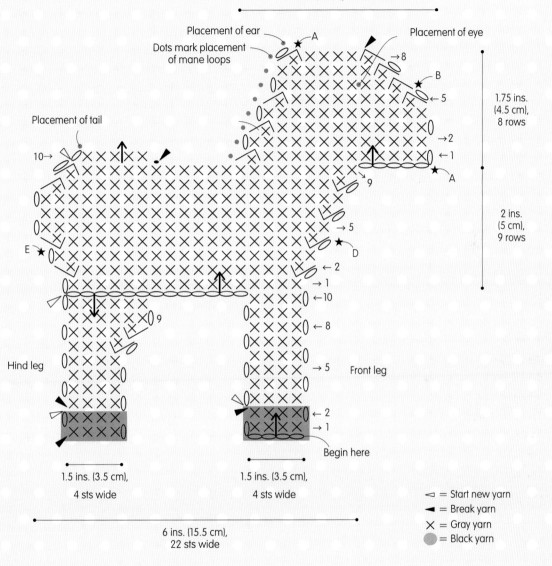

3.5 ins. (9 cm), 12 sts wide

Placement of ear

Dots mark placement
of mane loops

Placement of eye

→8

B

←5

1.75 ins.
(4.5 cm),
8 rows

Placement of tail

→2

→1

A

10→

2 ins.
(5 cm),
9 rows

9

→5

E ★

D

←2

→1

←10

←8

Hind leg

9

→5

Front leg

←2
→1

Begin here

1.5 ins. (3.5 cm),
4 sts wide

1.5 ins. (3.5 cm),
4 sts wide

◁ = Start new yarn

◀ = Break yarn

✕ = Gray yarn

● = Black yarn

6 ins. (15.5 cm),
22 sts wide

Donkey

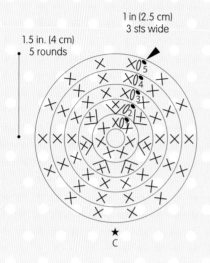

1 in (2.5 cm)
3 sts wide

1.5 in. (4 cm)
5 rounds

★
C

Muzzle:

Using the white yarn, begin with the crochet-in-the-round method by making a central ring. (See page 14 for detailed instructions.)

Round 1: sc 7 stitches around the loop. Pull the tail end of the yarn to tighten the center ring. Complete round 1 by making a sl st in the first sc of round.

Round 2: ch 1, sc inc in each st around. End with 14 sts. Sl st into first stitch of round.

Rounds 3–5: ch 1, sc 14, sl st in first sc of round. At the end of round 5, cut the yarn, leaving an 8-in. tail, then pull yarn through.

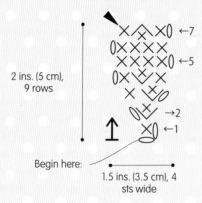

2 ins. (5 cm),
9 rows

Begin here:

1.5 ins. (3.5 cm), 4
sts wide

Ears (make two):

Using white yarn, begin with ch 2.

Row 1: Starting with the second chain from the hook, sc 1, ch 1.

Row 2: sc inc, ch 1.

Row 3: sc inc, sc 1, ch 1.

Row 4: sc 1, sc inc, sc 1, ch 1.

Row 5–6: sc 4, ch 1.

Row 7: sc 1, sc2tog, sc 1. Cut the yarn, leaving a 6-in. tail, then pull yarn through

Back of the Head:

Using the gray yarn, begin with ch 2 (one starting ch and one turning ch).

Row 1: Starting with the second chain from the hook, sc 1, ch 1.

Row 2: sc inc, then ch 1.

Row 3: sc 1, sc inc, ch 1.

Row 4: sc 1, sc inc, sc1, ch 1.

Rows 5–9: sc 4, ch 1. At the end of row 9, cut the yarn, leaving an 8-in. tail, then pull yarn through.

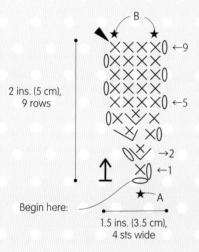

2 ins. (5 cm), 9 rows

Begin here:

1.5 ins. (3.5 cm), 4 sts wide

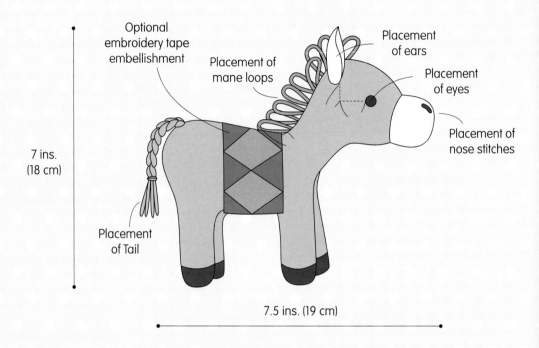

7 ins. (18 cm)

7.5 ins. (19 cm)

Optional embroidery tape embellishment

Placement of mane loops

Placement of ears

Placement of eyes

Placement of nose stitches

Placement of Tail

Tail:

Using the Main Body chart for placement, reattach the gray yarn at rump to begin tail. Ch 10. Cut yarn and pull through. Cut tip with about half inch left to untwist the yarn to resemble hair.

Face Details:

Using the medium-weight black yarn, make two straight stitches on the muzzle to make the nose. Add embroidered tapestry ribbon for embellishment, if desired.

Sew the Pieces Together:

Use the instructions on page 32 for how to assemble standing-style animals. Use the charts throughout the pattern for reference and piece placement. Before sewing up the back of the head, create mane by pulling new yarn through to make loops.

Nuts & Berries

These little accessories can be made up in blues and/or reds to make a little bunch of berries or in browns and tans for a tiny cluster of tree nuts just like the ones seen on page 40. The choice is yours.

Materials:

- Medium-weight yarn (acrylic and wool blend) in three colors (shown here: blue, purple, and navy for berries; brown, tan and dark brown for nuts), 3 yds each (1g)
- Medium-weight yarn (acrylic and wool blend) in green, 12 yds (4g)

Tools:

- US size G/6 (4.25 mm) crochet hook
- Tapestry or yarn needle
- Toy stuffing, small amount

Measurements:

Finished piece, berries: 4.75 x 2.5 ins. (12 x 6.5 cm); nuts: 2.5 x 2.5 ins. (6.5 x 6.5 cm).

*Note that measurements are approximate and will vary due to tension and yarn choice.

Pattern Notes:

This pattern is worked in the round for the berries and nuts, and flat for leaves. To make the figures as shown, you will create three berry/nut pieces. Make up three leaf pieces for the berry bunch, or two leaf pieces for the nut cluster. (Leaf pattern is found on page 93). It is then assembled with yarn and a tapestry needle, using the whipstitch.

Stitches Used:

Chain stitch (ch), single crochet (sc), single crochet increase (sc inc), single crochet decrease (sc2tog), slip stitch (sl st) and whipstitch. (See pages 10–13 for detailed instructions.)

Simply Adorable Crochet

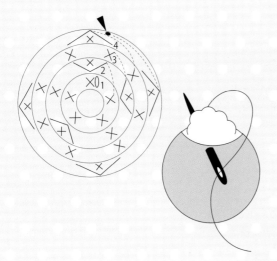

Berries or Nuts (make three):

Using the crochet-in-the- round method, make a center ring. (See page 14 for detailed instructions.)

Round 1: ch 1, sc 5. Begin each following round by crocheting into first stitch of previous round.

Round 2: (sc inc, sc 1) twice, sc inc.

Round 3: sc 8.

Round 4: (sc2tog) 4 times, sl st into first st of round; cut yarn, leaving an 8-in. tail, and pull through.

Repeat steps two more times in other colors to create the remaining berries or nuts.

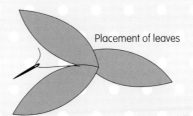

Placement of leaves

Finishing:

Make up the leaves as per the rose leaf instructions on page 93, then use the whipstitch to sew them together, referring to the diagrams above for placement. Stuff the berries or nuts with a small amount of toy stuffing. Weave yarn through the final round of berry and pull tight to close. Attach berries to leaves in a cluster. Weave in ends to finish.

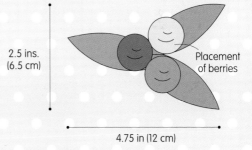

2.5 ins.
(6.5 cm)

Placement
of berries

4.75 in (12 cm)

Lamb

Materials:

- Bulky-weight yarn (acrylic and wool blend) in white, 60 yds (36g).
- Bulky-weight yarn with fuzzy texture (acrylic and nylon blend or mohair) in white, 30 yds (45 g). *Note: the fuzzier the yarn choice here, the woolier your sheep will look.*
- Medium-weight yarn (acrylic and wool blend) in black, small amount for detailing.

Tools:

- US size H/8 (5.0mm) crochet hook
- Tapestry or yarn needle
- Toy stuffing, 30g
- Sewing needle and cotton thread (if using buttons for eyes)
- Two black buttons or safety animal eyes (6 mm)

Measurements:

Finished piece is 6 x 6.25 x 3.5 ins. (15.5 x 16 x 8 cm)

Note that measurements are approximate and will vary due to tension and yarn choice.

Pattern Notes:

This pattern is worked flat, back and forth in single crochet, creating four main body pieces and three detailing pieces. It is then assembled afterwards with yarn and a tapestry needle using the whipstitch. This pattern can be tricky if you are using a fuzzy yarn. When choosing your yarn, know that the fuzzier it is, the harder it will be to see your stitches.

Stitches Used:

Crochet: chain stitch (ch), turning chain (tch), single crochet (sc), single crochet increase (sc inc), single crochet decrease (sc2tog), slip stitch (sl st). Piecing and details: whipstitch and embroidery. (See pages 10–13 for detailed crochet stitch instructions.)

Note: a ch 1 is at the end of every row. This is for the turning chain (tch), which is needed to begin the next row. The chart shows this at the beginning of each row.

Main Body, Head, Front and Hind Legs (make two):

Using plain, white yarn, begin with front leg: ch 4 (includes one for tch).

Row 1: Starting with the second chain from the hook, sc in each ch, 3 sc made. Ch 1.

Rows 2–8: Repeat row 1. At end of row, keep loop on hook. Front leg is completed.

Begin main body: switching to fuzzy white yarn, with loop remaining on hook, ch 15 (includes one for tch).

Row 1: Starting with the second chain from the hook, sc 17, ch 1. Be careful not to twist the chain when starting this row.

Row 2: sc inc, sc 15, sc inc in last ch. Ch 1.

Rows 3–7: sc 19, ch 1. Keep loop on hook, do not cut yarn.

Begin head and upper body:

Switching to plain white yarn, ch 4 (includes one for tch).

Row 1: sc 3, switch back to fuzzy white yarn, sc 17, sc2tog, ch 1.

Row 2: sc2tog, sc 16, switch to plain white yarn, sc 3, sc 1 for tch.

Row 3: sc 3, switch to fuzzy white yarn, sc 6, sc2tog, ch 1.

Row 4: sc 7, switch to plain white yarn, sc 3, ch 1.

Row 5: sc 3, switch to fuzzy white yarn, sc 7, ch 1.

Row 6: sc 7, switch to plain white yarn, sc 1, sc2tog, ch 1.

Row 7: sc2tog, switch to fuzzy white yarn, sc 5, sc2tog, ch 1.

Row 8: sc 5, sc2tog, ch 1.

Row 9: sc2tog, sc 2, sc2tog. Cut the yarn, leaving a 6-in. tail, then pull yarn through.

Begin hind leg as follows:

Reattach plain white yarn at the bottom end of body, opposite of front leg, ch 1 for starting ch.

Row 1: work sc in next 5 sts, ch 1.

Row 2: sc2tog, sc 3, ch 1.

Row 3: sc 2, sc2tog, ch 1.

Rows 4–8: sc 3, ch 1. At end of row 8, cut the yarn, leaving a 6-in. tail, then pull yarn through.

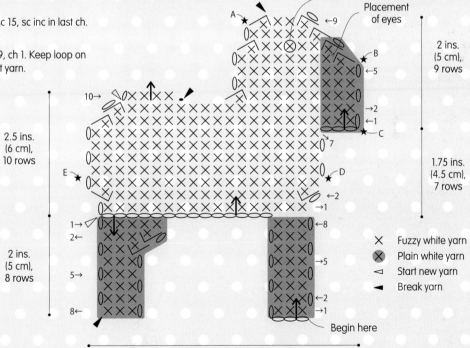

Placement of ears
Placement of eyes

2 ins. (5 cm), 9 rows

2.5 ins. (6 cm), 10 rows

1.75 ins. (4.5 cm), 7 rows

2 ins. (5 cm), 8 rows

Begin here

6.75 ins. (17 cm), 22 sts wide

✕ Fuzzy white yarn
⊗ Plain white yarn
◁ Start new yarn
◀ Break yarn

Underbody and Inner Legs:

Using the fuzzy white yarn, begin with ch 2 (one starting ch and one turning ch).

Row 1: Starting with the second chain from the hook, sc inc, ch 1.

Row 2: sc inc, sc 1, ch 1.

Rows 3–6: sc 3, ch 1.

Row 7: sc 1, sc inc, sc 1, ch 1.

Rows 8–13: sc 4, ch 1.

Row 14: sc 1, sc2tog, sc 1, ch 1.

Rows 15–18: sc 3, ch 1.

Row 19: sc 1, sc2tog, ch 1.

Row 20: sc2tog. Cut the yarn leaving a 6 in. tail, then pull yarn through. Belly section is complete.

Begin inner legs. Reattach plain white yarn at the fourth row of belly for first hind leg.

Row 1: Ch 1, sc 3 across side, ch 1.

Rows 2–8: sc 3, ch 1. At end of row 8, cut the yarn, leaving a 6-in. tail, pull yarn through.

Repeat these rows on opposite side of belly for second hind leg.

For front inner legs, reattach plain white yarn at row 15 of belly.

Row 1: ch 1, then sc 2 across side.

Rows 2–8: sc 2, ch 1. At the end of row 10, cut the yarn, leaving an 8-in. tail, then pull yarn through. Repeat these rows on opposite side of belly for second front leg. Underbody and inner legs are complete.

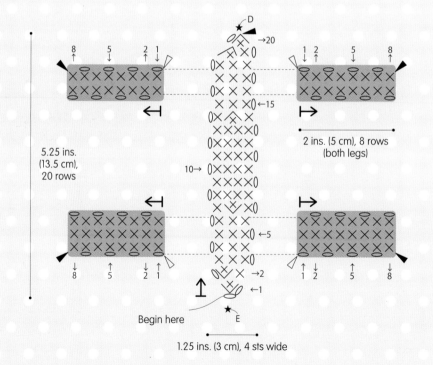

5.25 ins. (13.5 cm), 20 rows

2 ins. (5 cm), 8 rows (both legs)

Begin here

1.25 ins. (3 cm), 4 sts wide

Muzzle:

Using the plain white yarn, begin with the crochet-in-the-round method by making a slipknot for the central ring. (See page 14 for detailed instructions.)

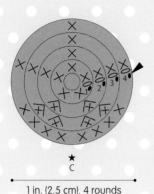

★
C

1 in. (2.5 cm), 4 rounds

Round 1: sc 5 stitches around the loop. Pull the tail end of the yarn to tighten the center ring. Complete round 1 by making a sl st in the first sc of row.

Round 2: ch 1, (sc 1, sc inc) twice, sc 1. Sl st into first stitch of round.

Round 3: ch1, (sc inc, sc 1) 3 times, sc inc. sl st into first stitch of round.

Round 4: ch 1, sc 11, sl st into first stitch of round. Cut the yarn, leaving an 8-in. tail, then pull yarn through. Muzzle is complete.

Back of Head:

Using the fuzzy white yarn, begin with ch 2 (one starting ch and one turning ch).

Row 1: Starting with the second chain from the hook, sc 1, ch 1.

Row 2: sc inc, ch 1.

Row 3: sc 1, sc inc, ch 1.

Row 4: sc 1, sc inc, sc1, ch 1.

Row 5: sc 1, sc inc, sc 2, ch 1.

Rows 6–7: sc 5, ch 1. At the end of row 7, cut the yarn, leaving a 6-in. tail. Switch to plain white yarn.

Row 8: sc 5, ch 1.

Row 9: sc2tog, sc 1, sc2tog. Cut the yarn, leaving an 8-in. tail, then pull yarn through.

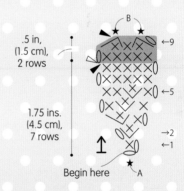

B

.5 in, (1.5 cm), 2 rows

←9

←5

1.75 ins. (4.5 cm), 7 rows

→2
←1

Begin here

A

X	Fuzzy white yarn
⊗	Plain white yarn
◁	Start new yarn
◀	Break yarn

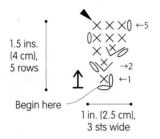

1.5 ins.
(4 cm),
5 rows

←5
→2
←1

Begin here

1 in. (2.5 cm),
3 sts wide

Ears (make two):

Using fuzzy white yarn, begin with ch 2.

Row 1: Starting with the second chain from the hook, sc 1, ch 1.

Row 2: sc inc, ch 1.

Row 3: sc inc, sc 1, ch 1.

Rows 4–5: sc 3. Cut the yarn, leaving an 8-in. tail, then pull yarn through.

Sew the Pieces Together:

Use the instructions on page 32 for how to assemble standing-style animals. Use the charts throughout the pattern for reference and piece placement. When attaching ears, fold them slightly to give them shape.

Face Details:

Using the black yarn and tapestry needle, embroider two straight stitches to create the mouth and another two to create the nose.

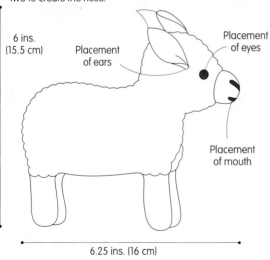

6 ins.
(15.5 cm)

Placement
of ears

Placement
of eyes

Placement
of mouth

6.25 ins. (16 cm)

Daisy

Materials:

- Medium-weight yarn (acrylic and wool blend) in white and blue, 6 yds (2g) each
- Medium-weight yarn (acrylic and wool blend) in green, 3 yds (1g)
- Medium-weight yarn (acrylic and wool blend in yellow, 3 yds (1g)

Tools:

- US size G/6 (4.25 mm) crochet hook
- Tapestry or yarn needle

Measurements:

Finished piece is 3.25 x 2.25 ins. (8.5 x 6 cm)

Note that measurements are approximate and will vary due to tension and yarn choice.

Pattern Notes:

This pattern is worked in the round for the flower center, and the petals flat with connecting slip stitches. The leaf is worked flat. It is then assembled afterwards with yarn and a tapestry needle using the whipstitch.

Stitches Used:

Chain stitch (ch), single crochet (sc), half-double crochet (hdc), slip stitch (sl st) and whipstitch. (See pages 10–13 for detailed instructions.)

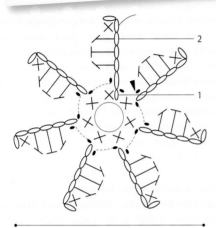

2.25 ins. (6 cm)

◄ Break yarn

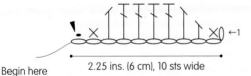

Begin here

2.25 ins. (6 cm), 10 sts wide

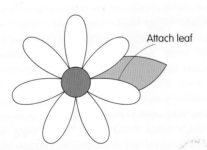

Attach leaf

Flower:

Using yellow yarn and the crochet-in-the-round method, make a center ring. (See page 14 for detailed instructions.)

Center round: ch 1, sc 7. Sl st into first stitch of round, then switch to blue or white yarn.

Petals: Ch 6.

Sc in second chain from hook, hdc 3, sl st. Sl st again into next stitch of center round. Repeat six more times for all petals.

Sl st into first stitch of round; cut yarn, leaving a 6-in. tail, and pull through.

Leaf:

Using green yarn, begin with ch 11.

Row 1: Starting with second chain from hook, sc 1, hdc 2, dc 4, hdc 1, sc 1, sl st. Cut yarn, leaving a 6-in. tail, and pull through.

Sew the Pieces Together:

Use the whipstitch to attach leaf to back of daisy, if desired.

Into the Woods

Bunny

Materials:

- Bulky-weight yarn (acrylic and wool blend) in white, 80 yds (50g)
- Medium-weight yarn (acrylic and wool blend) in pink, small amount for nose details.

Tools:

- US size H/8 (5.0mm) crochet hook
- Tapestry or yarn needle
- Toy stuffing, 30g
- Sewing needle and cotton thread (if using buttons for eyes)
- Two black buttons or safety animal eyes (9 mm)

Measurements:

Finished piece is 4 x 8.5 x 2.75 ins. (10 x 22 x 7 cm)

Note that measurements are approximate and will vary due to tension and yarn choice.

Pattern Notes:

This pattern is worked flat, back and forth in single crochet, creating four main body pieces and two detailing pieces. It is then assembled afterwards with yarn and a tapestry needle using the whipstitch.

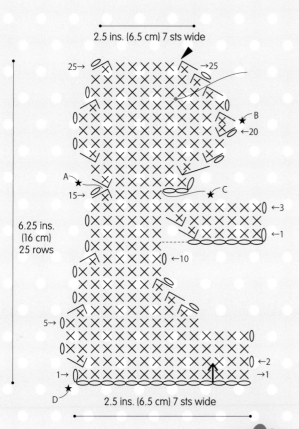

2.5 ins. (6.5 cm) 7 sts wide

6.25 ins. (16 cm) 25 rows

2.5 ins. (6.5 cm) 7 sts wide

Main Body, Head, Upper and Lower Legs (make two):

Begin with ch 15 (includes one for tch).

Row 1: Begin with second chain from hook, sc 14, ch 1.

Row 2: sc 13, sc inc, ch 1.

Rows 3–4: sc 15, ch 1.

Row 5: sc 11, ch 1, turn before reaching end of piece.

Row 6: sc2tog, sc 7, sc2tog, ch 1.

Row 7: sc 7, sc2tog, ch 1.

Row 8: sc2tog, sc 6, ch 1.

Row 9: sc 7, ch 1.

Row 10: sc 5, sc2tog, ch 1.

Rows 11–13: sc 6, ch 1. At the end of row 13, cut yarn, leaving a 6-in. tail and pull through.

Begin arm with ch 7 (includes one for tch).

Row 1: sc 5, sc inc, ch 1.

Row 2: sc inc, sc 6, ch 1.

Row 3: sc 8, reattach to body by continuing sc across the top of body piece.

Sc 6, ch 1. (Row now becomes row 14 on chart).

Continue with head.

Row 15: sc2tog, sc 4, ch 3.

Row 16: sc 6, sc inc, ch 1.

Row 17: sc 7, sc3inc in next stitch (triple increase made), ch 1.

Row 18: sc inc, sc 8, sc inc, ch 1.

Row 19: sc 12, ch 1.

Row 20: sc inc, sc 11, ch 1.

Row 21: sc 11, sc2tog, ch 1.

Row 22: sc 10, sc2tog, ch 1.

Row 23: sc 9, sc2tog, ch 1.

Row 24: sc2tog, sc 8, ch 1.

Row 25: sc2tog, sc 5, sc2tog. Cut yarn, leaving 6-in. tail, and pull through.

Stitches Used:

Crochet: chain stitch (ch), turning chain (tch), single crochet (sc), single crochet increase (sc inc), single crochet decrease (sc2tog), slip stitch (sl st). Piecing and details: whipstitch and embroidery. (See pages 10–13 for detailed crochet stitch instructions.)

Special stitch used for this figure—single crochet triple Increase (sc3inc): single crochet three times into the same stitch.

Note: a ch 1 is at the end of every row. This is for the turning chain (tch), which is needed to begin the next row. The chart shows this at the beginning of each row.

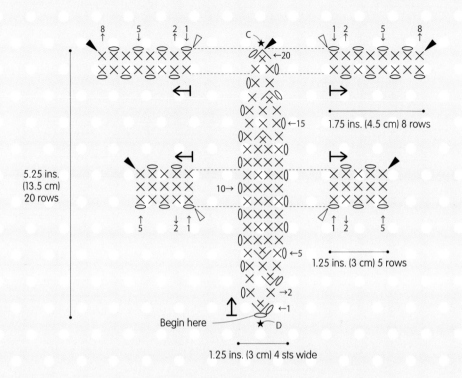

5.25 ins.
(13.5 cm)
20 rows

1.75 ins. (4.5 cm) 8 rows

1.25 ins. (3 cm) 5 rows

Begin here

1.25 ins. (3 cm) 4 sts wide

Underbody and Inner Legs:

Begin with ch 2 (one starting ch and one turning ch.)

Row 1: Starting with the second chain from the hook, sc 1, ch 1.

Row 2: sc inc, ch 1.

Row 3: sc inc, sc 1, ch 1.

Row 4: sc 3, ch 1.

Row 5: sc 1, sc inc, sc 1, ch 1.

Rows 6–13: sc 4, ch 1.

Row 14: sc 1, sc2tog, sc 1, ch 1.

Rows 15–16: sc 3, ch 1.

Row 17: sc2tog, sc 1, ch 1.

Rows 18–19: sc 2, ch 1.

Row 20: sc2tog. Cut the yarn leaving a 6-in. tail, then pull yarn through. Underbelly section is complete.

Begin inner legs. Reattach yarn at the ninth row of belly for first lower leg.

Row 1: Ch 1, sc 3 across side, ch 1.

Rows 2–5: sc 3, ch 1. At the end of row 5, cut the yarn, leaving an 8-in. tail, then pull yarn through.

Repeat these rows on opposite side of belly for second lower leg.

Reattach yarn at the end of belly for first upper leg.

Row 1: Ch 1, sc 2 across side, ch 1.

Rows 2–8: sc 2, ch 1. At the end of row 8, cut the yarn leaving an 8 in. tail, then pull yarn through.

Repeat these rows on opposite side of belly for second upper leg.

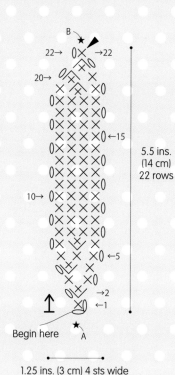

B
22→ →22
20→
←15
10→
←5
→2
←1

5.5 ins.
(14 cm)
22 rows

Begin here
A

1.25 ins. (3 cm) 4 sts wide

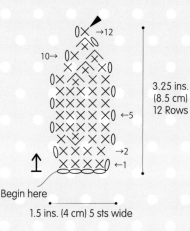

→12
10→
←5
→2
←1

3.25 ins.
(8.5 cm)
12 Rows

Begin here

1.5 ins. (4 cm) 5 sts wide

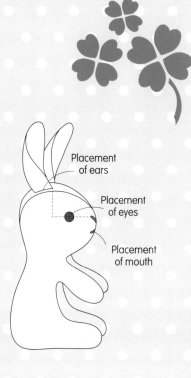

Placement
of ears

Placement
of eyes

Placement
of mouth

Back of Head:

Begin with ch 2 (one starting ch and one turning ch).

Row 1: Starting with the second chain from the hook, sc 1, ch 1.

Row 2: sc inc, ch 1.

Row 3: sc 2, ch 1.

Row 4: sc inc, ch 1.

Row 5: sc 3, ch 1.

Row 6: sc 1, sc inc, sc 1, ch 1.

Rows 7–18: sc 4, ch 1.

Row 19: sc 1, sc2tog, sc 1, ch 1.

Row 20: sc2tog, sc 1, ch 1.

Row 21: sc2tog, ch 1.

Row 22: sc 1. Cut the yarn leaving an 8-in. tail, then pull yarn through.

Ears (make two):

Begin with ch 5 (includes one for tch).

Rows 1–2: sc 4, ch 1.

Row 3: sc 2, sc inc, sc 1, ch 1.

Rows 4–7: sc 5, ch 1.

Row 8: sc 1, sc2tog, sc 2, ch 1.

Row 9: sc 1, sc2tog, sc 1, ch 1.

Row 10: sc 1, sc2tog, ch 1.

Row 11: sc2tog, ch 1.

Row 12: sc 1. Cut the yarn, leaving an 8-in. tail, then pull yarn through.

Sew the Pieces Together:

Use the instructions on page 32 for how to assemble figures. Use the charts throughout the pattern for reference and piece placement.

Fold ears in half to give them shape. Use straight stitches with pink yarn for nose and mouth details.

Strawberries

Materials:

- Medium-weight yarn (acrylic and wool blend) in pink or red, 7 yds (3g)
- Medium-weight yarn (acrylic and wool blend) in green, 3 yds (1g)
- Medium-weight yarn (acrylic and wool blend) in white, 3 yds (1g)

Tools:

- US size G/6 (4.25 mm) crochet hook
- Tapestry or yarn needle
- Toy stuffing, small amount
- Locking stitch marker

Measurements:

Finished piece, 2 x 1.25 in. (5 x 3 cm)

Note that measurements are approximate and will vary due to tension and yarn choice.

Pattern Notes:

This pattern is worked in the round for the berry and flat for the leafy top. It is then assembled afterwards with yarn and a tapestry needle using the whipstitch. The simplified pattern without the step-by-step instructions is also included here.

Stitches Used:

Crochet: chain stitch (ch), double crochet (dc), single crochet (sc), single crochet increase (sc inc), single crochet decrease (sc2tog) and slip stitch (sl st). Piecing and details: whipstitch. (See pages 10–13 for detailed stitch instructions.)

Ball-shaped objects like fruits and nuts are crocheted continually in the round by crocheting over a loop called the center ring. Crocheting in the round is useful for creating shapes in three dimensions. Just by changing the number of stitches and rows, you can make a variety of different round shapes.

To make a seamless ball, do not work a slip stitch at the end of each row. Simply crochet into the first stitch of the last round to create a continuous spiral. By using a locking stitch marker on the first stitch of each round, you can easily keep track of your rounds.

This strawberry, a simple accessory that can be used for any of the woodland creature projects, makes an ideal showcase for the crochet-in-the-round technique.

Work in a Continuous Spiral:

1 Make a single loop, insert a hook into the loop from front to back and draw up a loop. This creates the center ring.

2 **Round 1:** Work a chain stitch as a starting chain, then work a single crochet.

3 Continue to crochet over the loop, sc 6 total.

4 Hold the yarn tail and pull to draw the center ring tightly closed. This completes round 1.

5 Work sc inc at seventh stitch as starting stitch of second row. Place your locking stitch marker in the first stitch of a new round to help keep track of your rounds. Important: Do not join with a sl st at the end of each round and work in a continuous spiral.

6 **Round 2:** (sc inc) six times (including the first of the round).

Special Decorative Details:

7 **Round 3:** (sc 1 in white, sc 3 in red) three times. Create the white spots using the technique as follows: yarn over with white yarn and pull the yarn through from the first stitch of the third row.

8 Then, switch to red yarn. Yarn over and pull through loops.

9 This will create the V-shaped spots (the seeds) on your strawberry (and on the mushroom). Sc 3 with red, repeat steps 7–9 for the next spot.

10 Repeat 4 stitches once more to complete third round.

11 **Round 4:** (sc 1, sc inc) six times.

Round 5: sc 4 in red, sc 1 in white, (sc 5 in red, sc 1 in white) twice, sc 1.

Round 6: sc 18.

Round 7: sc 1, (sc 1 in white, sc 5 in red) twice, sc 1 in white, sc 4 in red.

White yarn inside piece will appear like this.

12 Continue to crochet over the loop, sc 6 total.

13 Leaving an 8-in. tail, break the yarn. Stuff the strawberry with toy stuffing.

14 Weave the tail in and out of the last round.

15 Pull the yarn tight to tighten the top of strawberry. Fasten off and weave in end.

Completed berry

Using Crochet in the Round for Finishing Details:

16 Make a center ring, crochet over the loop. **Round 1:** ch 1, sc 5.

17 Pull the starting end of the yarn tight to close the center ring. Insert hook into first single crochet and work sl st. First row is complete.

18 **Round 2:** ch 3 for starting chain. Dc 1 in to first stitch of previous row as follows: begin with a yarn over.

Using Crochet in the Round for Finishing Details:

19 Insert hook into first starting chain stitch, yarn over and pull through.

20 Yarn over and pull through two loops.

21 Yarn over again and pull through the remaining loops.

22 Double crochet is completed.

23 To finish round 2, ch 3, sl st through second stitch of previous row. First leaf is complete.

24 Repeat four more times to make five leaves as shown (use the crochet chart for stitch placement reference). Cut the yarn, leaving an 8-in. tail.

Sew the Pieces Together:

25 Flip over the leaves. Make a loop by using starting end of yarn and pulling through the center and fasten off the yarn.

26 Pass end yarn of the leafy top through the yarn needle. Attach berry to the top using the whipstitch underneath the top.

27 Repeat four more times to make five leafy tops as shown.

Berry:

Using red or pink yarn and the crochet-in-the round method, make a center ring.

Round 1: ch 1, sc 6. Begin each following round by crocheting into first stitch of previous round. Mark first stitch with a locking stitch marker to indicate the beginning of your rounds.

Round 2: (sc inc) six times.

Round 3: (sc 1 in white, sc 3 in red) three times. (See photo section on making white spots.)

Round 4: (sc 1, sc inc) six times.

Round 5: sc 4 in red, sc 1 in white, (sc 5 in red, sc 1 in white) twice, sc 1.

Round 6: sc 18.

Round 7: sc 1, (sc 1 in white, sc 5 in red) twice, sc 1 in white, sc 4 in red.

Round 8: (sc 1, sc2tog) six times.

Round 9: (sc2tog) six times.

Leafy Top:

Using green yarn and the crochet-in-the round method, make a center ring.

Round 1: ch 1, sc 6, sl st.

Round 2: ch 3, dc 1 in to first stitch of previous row, ch 3, sl st into next stitch. Repeat four more times to finish leaves.

Finishing the Berry:

Pull a loop through the center of the leafy top for stem and fasten off underneath. Stuff the berry with toy stuffing, weave tail around top row, and pull tight to close. Use the whipstitch to attach leaves to berry and weave in any ends to finish your strawberry.

Want to make strawberry blossoms? Follow the leafy top pattern, using yellow for round one and white for round two!

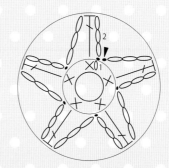

Mushrooms

Materials:

- Bulky-weight yarn (acrylic and wool blend) in dark brown or some other woodsy color, 25 yds (15g)
- Bulky-weight yarn (acrylic and wool blend) in tan, 7 yds (4g)
- Bulky-weight yarn (acrylic and wool blend) in white, 2 yds (1g)

Tools:

- US size H/8 (4.25 mm) crochet hook
- Tapestry or yarn needle
- Toy stuffing, small amount
- Locking stitch marker

Measurements:

Finished piece is 3.5 x 3 ins. (9 x 7.5 cm)

*Note that measurements are approximate and will vary due to tension and yarn choice.

Stitches Used:

Crochet: chain stitch (ch), single crochet (sc), single crochet increase (sc inc), single crochet decrease (sc2tog) and slip stitch (sl st). Piecing: Whipstitch. (See pages 10–13 for detailed instructions.)

Pattern Notes:

This pattern is worked in the round for both the cap and stalk. It is then assembled afterwards with yarn and a tapestry needle using the whipstitch.

Cap:

Using dark brown yarn and the crochet-in-the-round method, make a center ring. (See page 14 for detailed instructions.)

Round 1: ch 1, sc 5. Begin each following round by crocheting into first stitch of previous round. Mark first stitch of each new round with a locking stitch marker.

Round 2: (sc inc) 5 times.

Round 3: (sc 1, sc inc) 5 times.

Round 4: (sc 1 in white, sc 1, sc inc) 5 times. (See page 45 for how to sew white spots.)

Round 5: (sc 3, sc inc) 5 times.

Round 6: (sc 4, sc inc) 5 times.

Round 7: (sc 3, sc 1 in white, sc 1, sc inc) 5 times.

Rounds 8–9: sc 35.

Round 10: (sc 1 in white, sc 6) 5 times.

Round 11: sc 35.

Round 12: (sc2tog, sc 3) 7 times.

Round 13: (sc2tog, sc 2) 7 times. Stuff cap with toy stuffing now before finishing last two rounds.

Round 14: (sc2tog, sc 1) 7 times.

Round 15: (sc2tog) 7 times, sl st. Cut yarn, leaving an 8-in. tail, and pull through.

Fill top with rest of toy stuffing to desired firmness.

Stalk:

Using tan yarn and the crochet-in-the-round method, make center ring. (See page 14 for detailed instructions.)

Round 1: ch 1, sc 8. Begin each following round by crocheting into first stitch of previous round. Mark first stitch of each new round with a locking stitch marker.

Round 2: sc 1, (sc inc) 7 times.

Rounds 3–5: sc 15.

Round 6: (sc2tog, sc 2) 4 times, sc 1.

Rounds 7–8: sc 11, sl st. Cut yarn, leaving an 8-in. tail, and pull through.

Stuff stalk with toy stuffing. Don't overstuff; you want to be able to keep the bottom flat so mushroom can stand.

Finishing Details:

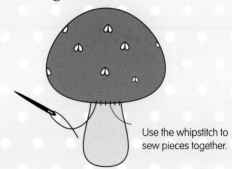

Use the whipstitch to sew pieces together.

Squirrel

Materials:

- Bulky-weight yarn (acrylic and wool blend) in tan, 64 yds (40g)
- Bulky-weight yarn (acrylic and wool blend) in brown, 10 yds (5g)
- Bulky-weight yarn (acrylic and wool blend) in white, 10 yds (5g)
- Medium-weight yarn in dark brown yarn for nose details, small amount

Tools:

- US size H/8 (5.0mm) crochet hook
- Tapestry or yarn needle
- Sewing needle and cotton thread (if using buttons for eyes)
- Toy stuffing, 30g
- Two black buttons or safety animal eyes (9 mm)

Stitches Used:

Crochet: chain stitch (ch), turning chain (tch), single crochet (sc), single crochet increase (sc inc), single crochet decrease (sc2tog), slip stitch (sl st). Piecing and details: whipstitch and embroidery. (See pages 10–13 for detailed instructions.)

Pattern: *Note: a ch 1 is at the end of every row. This is for the turning chain (tch), which is needed to begin the next row. The chart shows this at the beginning of each row.*

Measurements:

Finished piece is 6 x 5.5 x 3 ins. (15.5 x 14 x 7.5 cm)

Note that measurements are approximate and will vary due to tension and yarn choice.

Pattern Notes:

This pattern is worked flat, back and forth in single crochet, creating four main body pieces and four detailing pieces. It is then assembled afterwards with yarn and a tapestry needle using the whipstitch.

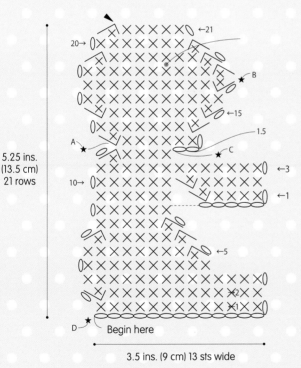

5.25 ins.
(13.5 cm)
21 rows

3.5 ins. (9 cm) 13 sts wide

Main Body, Head, Upper and Lower Legs (make two):

Using brown yarn, begin with ch 14 (includes one for tch).

Row 1: Begin with second chain from hook, sc 13, ch 1.

Row 2: sc inc, sc 12, ch 1.

Row 3: sc 14, ch 1.

Row 4: sc 10, ch 1; turn before reaching end of piece.

Row 5: sc2tog, sc 7, sc2tog, ch 1.

Row 6: sc2tog, sc 5, sc2tog, ch 1.

Row 7: sc2tog, sc 5, ch 1.

Rows 8–10: sc 6, ch 1. At the end of row 10, cut yarn, leaving a 6-inch tail, and pull through.

Begin arm with ch 6. (includes one for tch)

Row 1: sc 4, sc inc, ch 1.

Row 2: sc inc, sc 5, ch 1.

Row 3: sc 7, reattach to body by continuing sc across the top of body piece.

Sc 6, ch 1. (Row now becomes row 11 on chart.)

Continue with head.

Row 12: sc2tog, sc 4, ch 3. (includes one for tch)

Row 13: sc 6, sc inc, ch 1.

Row 14: sc 7, sc inc, ch 1.

Row 15: sc inc, sc 7, sc inc, ch 1.

Row 16: sc 11, ch 1.

Row 17: sc inc, sc 10, ch 1.

Row 18: sc 10, sc2tog, ch 1.

Row 19: sc2tog, sc 7, sc2tog, ch 1.

Row 20: sc 7, sc2tog, ch 1.

Row 21: skip first stitch, sc 5, sc2tog. Cut yarn, leaving 6-in. tail, and pull though.

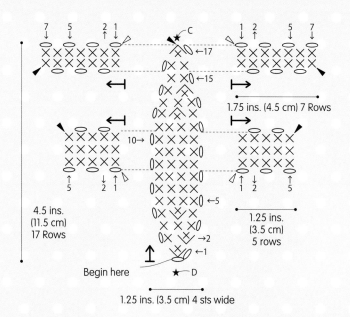

1.75 ins. (4.5 cm) 7 Rows

4.5 ins.
(11.5 cm)
17 Rows

1.25 ins.
(3.5 cm)
5 rows

Begin here ★—D

1.25 ins. (3.5 cm) 4 sts wide

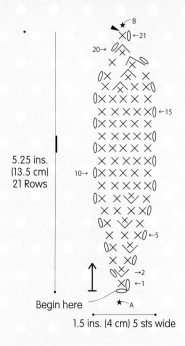

5.25 ins.
(13.5 cm)
21 Rows

Begin here ★—A

1.5 ins. (4 cm) 5 sts wide

Underbody and Inner Legs:

Using white yarn, begin with ch 2 (one starting ch and one turning ch).

Row 1: Starting with the second chain from the hook, sc inc, ch 1.

Row 2: sc 1, sc inc, ch 1.

Row 3: sc 3, ch 1.

Row 4: sc 1 sc inc, sc 1, ch 1.

Rows 5–11: sc 4, ch 1.

Row 12: sc 1 sc2tog, sc 1, ch 1.

Row 13: sc 3, ch 1.

Row 14: sc 1, sc2tog, ch 1.

Rows 15–16: sc 2, ch 1.

Row 17: sc2tog. Cut the yarn leaving a 6-in. tail, then pull yarn through. Belly section is complete.

Begin inner legs. Reattach yarn at the eighth row of belly for first lower leg.

Row 1: Ch 1, sc 3 across side, ch 1.

Rows 2–5: sc 3, ch 1. At the end of row 5, cut the yarn, leaving an 8-in. tail, then pull yarn through.

Repeat these rows on opposite side of belly for second lower leg.

Reattach yarn at the end of belly for first upper leg.

Row 1: ch 1, sc 2 across side, ch 1.

Rows 2–8: sc 2, ch 1. At the end of row 7, cut the yarn leaving an 8-in. tail, then pull yarn through.

Repeat these rows on opposite side of belly for second upper leg.

Back of Head:

Using tan yarn, begin with ch 2 (one starting ch and one turning ch).

Row 1: Starting with the second chain from the hook, sc 1, ch 1.

Row 2: sc inc, ch 1.

Row 3: sc 2, ch 1.

Row 4: sc 1, sc inc, ch 1.

Row 5: sc 3, ch 1.

Row 6: sc 1, sc inc, sc 1, ch 1.

Row 7: sc 4, ch 1.

Row 8: sc 2, sc inc, sc 1, ch 1.

Rows 9–16: sc 5, ch 1.

Row 17: sc 2, sc2tog, sc 1, ch 1.

Row 18: sc 1, sc2tog, sc 1, ch 1.

Row 19: sc2tog, sc 1, ch 1.

Row 20: sc2tog, ch 1.

Row 21: sc 1. Cut the yarn, leaving an 8-in. tail, then pull yarn through.

Ears (make two):

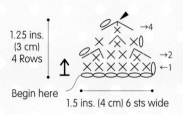

1.25 ins. (3 cm) 4 Rows

Begin here

1.5 ins. (4 cm) 6 sts wide

Using tan yarn, begin with ch 7 (includes one for tch).

Row 1: starting with the second chain from the hook, sc 6, ch 1.

Row 2: sc2tog, sc 2, sc2tog, ch 1.

Row 3: sc 1, sc2tog, sc 1, ch 1.

Nose Tip:

Using medium-weight brown yarn, ch 2.

Row 1: sc 2 into the second chain from hook. Cut yarn, leaving an 8-in. tail, and pull through.

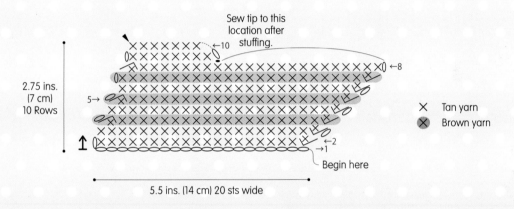

Sew tip to this location after stuffing.

2.75 ins. (7 cm) 10 Rows

Begin here

5.5 ins. (14 cm) 20 sts wide

✕ Tan yarn
⊗ Brown yarn

Tail (make two):

Using tan yarn, begin with ch 21 (includes one for tch).

Row 1: sc 19, sc inc, ch 1.

Row 2: sc inc, sc 20, switch to brown yarn, ch 1.

Row 3 (brown): sc2tog, sc 19, sc inc, switch to tan yarn, ch 1.

Row 4 (tan): sc inc, sc 21, switch to brown yarn, ch 1.

Row 5 (brown): sc2tog, sc 20, sc inc, switch to tan yarn, ch 1.

Row 6 (tan): sc inc, sc 22, switch to brown yarn, ch 1.

Row 7 (brown): sc 23, sc inc, switch to tan yarn, ch 1.

Row 8 (tan): sc 23, sc2tog, ch 1.

Row 9: sc 8, ch 1.

Row 10: skip first stitch, sc 7. Cut the yarn, leaving an 8-in. tail, then pull yarn through.

Repeat entire sequence for second half of tail.

5.5 ins.
(14 cm)

Placement
of ears

Placement
of eyes

Placement of
nose tip and
mouth details

Attach tail here

6 ins. (15.5 cm)

Sewing Pieces Together:

Affix safety eyes, if using, at this point, following package instructions (consult chart for placement).

Use the instructions on page 32 for how to assemble figures. Use the charts throughout the pattern for reference and piece placement.

Sew two tail pieces together using the whipstitch. Fill tail with toy stuffing 80% of the way before closing up completely. Bend tip of tail down to a point in back of tail, then use one stitch to sew together to give the tail its shape.

Finishing Details:

Attach tail to back of body after main body has been stuffed. Fold ears in half to give them shape when attaching. Attach nose tip with whipstitch, using tails of yarn from nose tip. Sew on buttons for eyes at this point, if using. Using brown yarn, make straight stitches for mouth details.

Simply Adorable Crochet

Acorns

Materials:

- Medium-weight yarn (acrylic and wool blend) in tan and brown, 3 yds (1g) each

Tools:

- US size G/6 (4.25 mm) crochet hook
- Tapestry or yarn needle
- Toy stuffing, small amount
- Locking stitch marker

Stitches Used:

Crochet: chain stitch (ch), single crochet (sc), single crochet increase (sc inc), single crochet decrease (sc2tog) and slip stitch (sl st). Piecing: whipstitch. (See pages 10–13 for detailed instructions.)

Measurements:

Finished piece is 1.75 x 1 ins. (4.5 x 2.5 cm)

*Note that measurements are approximate and will vary due to tension and yarn choice.

Pattern Notes:

This pattern is worked in the round for both the nut and cap. It is then assembled afterwards with yarn and a tapestry needle using the whipstitch.

Simply Adorable Crochet

Nut:

Using tan yarn and the crochet-in-the-round method, make a center ring. (See page 14 for detailed instructions.)

Round 1: ch 1, sc 4. Begin each following round by crocheting into first stitch of previous round. Mark first stitch of each new round with a locking stitch marker.

Round 2: (sc inc, sc 1) twice.

Round 3: (sc 1, sc inc) 3 times.

Round 4: sc 9.

Round 5: (sc 2, sc inc) 3 times.

Round 6: sc 12.

Round 7: (sc 1, sc2tog) 4 times. Cut yarn, leaving an 8-in. tail, and pull through.

Cap:

Using brown yarn and the crochet-in-the-round method, make a center ring.

Round 1: ch 1, sc 6. Begin each following round by crocheting into first stitch of previous round. Mark first stitch of each new round with a locking stitch marker.

Round 2: (sc inc) 6 times.

Round 3: sc 4, sc inc, sc 5, sc inc, sc 1.

Round 4: sc 14. Cut yarn, leaving an 8-in. tail, and pull through.

Flip cap inside out to create the curve of acorn. Use starting end of yarn to make a loop for the cap stem.

Finishing Details:

Use the whipstitch to sew pieces together.

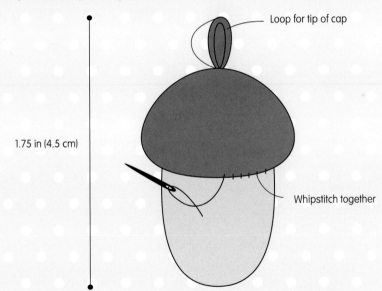

Loop for tip of cap

1.75 in (4.5 cm)

Whipstitch together

Mr. & Mrs. Bear

Materials:

- Bulky-weight yarn (acrylic and wool blend) in white for bride, 80 yds (50g)
- Bulky-weight yarn (acrylic and wool blend) in light brown for groom, 80 yds (50g)
- Medium-weight yarn (acrylic and wool blend) in black, 6 yds (2g) for bow tie
- Medium-weight gray yarn, small amount for nose details
- Tulle or lace, 7 x 20-in. piece for veil details

Tools:

- US size H/8 (5.0mm) crochet hook
- US size D/3 (3.25mm) crochet hook
- Tapestry or yarn needle
- Toy stuffing, 30g
- Sewing needle and cotton thread (if using buttons for eyes)
- Two black buttons or safety animal eyes (9 mm)

Stitches Used:

Crochet: chain stitch (ch), turning chain (tch), single crochet (sc), single crochet increase (sc inc), single crochet decrease (sc2tog), slip stitch (sl st). Piecing and details: whipstitch and embroidery. (See pages 10–13 for detailed instructions.)

Note: a ch 1 is at the end of every row. This is for the turning chain (tch), which is needed to begin the next row. The chart shows this at the beginning of each row.

Measurements:

Finished piece is 7.5 x 4 x 4 ins. (19 x 10 x 10 cm)

Note that measurements are approximate and will vary due to tension and yarn choice.

Pattern Notes:

This pattern is worked flat, back and forth in single crochet, creating four main body pieces and four detailing pieces. Arms are crocheted in the round separately from the main body pieces. Roses and bow tie are crocheted separately. It is then assembled afterwards with yarn and a tapestry needle using the whipstitch.

Main Body, Head, Upper and Lower Legs (make two):

Begin with ch 16 (includes one for tch).

Row 1: Begin with second chain from hook, sc 14, ch 1.

Row 2: sc inc, sc 14, ch 1.

Rows 3–5: sc 16, ch 1.

Row 6: sc 12, ch 1, turn before reaching end of piece.

Row 7: sc2tog, sc 8, sc2tog, ch

Rows 8–10: sc 10, ch 1.

Row 11: sc2tog, sc 8, ch 1.

Rows 12–15: sc 9, ch 1.

Row 16: sc2tog, sc 7, ch 1.

Row 17: sc inc, sc 6, sc inc, ch 1

Row 18: sc 9, sc inc, ch 1.

Row 19: (sc inc) twice, sc 9, ch 1

Rows 20–23: sc 13, ch 1.

Row 24: sc 7, sc2tog, ch 1, turn before reaching end of piece.

Row 25: sc 6, sc2tog, ch 1.

Row 26: sc 5, sc2tog, ch 1.

Row 27: sc2tog, sc 2, sc2tog. Cut yarn, leaving a 6-in. tail, and pull through.

Use a locking stitch marker to indicate where the arms should be attached now. It will make it much easier to find the right spot when you are ready to place them later!

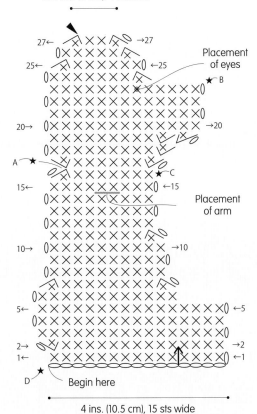

1.25 ins. (3 cm,) 4 stitches

Placement of eyes

Placement of arm

Begin here

4 ins. (10.5 cm), 15 sts wide

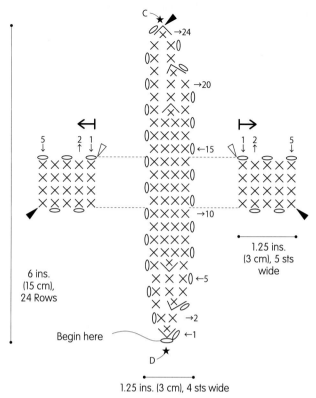

6 ins.
(15 cm),
24 Rows

Begin here

1.25 ins. (3 cm), 4 sts wide

1.25 ins.
(3 cm), 5 sts
wide

Underbody and Inner Legs:

Begin with ch 2 (one starting ch and one turning ch).

Row 1: Starting with the second chain from the hook, sc inc, ch 1.

Row 2: sc 2, ch 1.

Row 3: sc inc, sc 2, ch 1.

Rows 4–5: sc 3, ch 1.

Row 6: sc 1 sc inc, sc 1, ch 1.

Rows 7–17: sc 4, ch 1.

Row 18: sc 1 sc2tog, sc 1, ch 1.

Rows 19–20: sc 3, ch 1.

Row 21: sc2tog, sc 1, ch 1.

Rows 22–23: sc 2, ch 1.

Row 24: sc2tog. Cut the yarn, leaving a 6-in. tail, then pull yarn through.

Begin inner legs. Reattach yarn at the fifteenth row of belly for first lower leg.

Row 1: ch 1, sc 4 across side, ch 1.

Rows 2–5: sc 4, ch 1. At the end of row 5, cut the yarn, leaving an 8-in. tail, then pull yarn through.

Repeat these rows on opposite side of belly for second lower leg.

Nose Tip:

Using medium-weight gray yarn, ch 2.

Row 1: sc inc. Cut the yarn leaving an 8-in. tail, then pull yarn through.

Be sure to leave long tails to use for sewing face details.

Ears (make two):

Using crochet-in-the-round method, make a center ring.

Round 1: ch 1, sc 5, ch 1. Do not join with sl st. Turn and work back and forth to create the ear shape.

Round 2: (sc 1, sc inc) twice, sc 1, ch 1.

Round 3: (sc 1, sc inc) three times, sc 1. Cut the yarn, leaving an 8-in. tail, then pull yarn through.

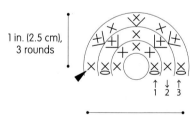

1 in. (2.5 cm),
3 rounds

1.75 in. (3.8 cm), 6 sts wide

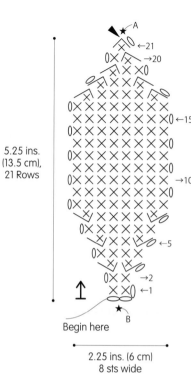

5.25 ins.
(13.5 cm),
21 Rows

2.25 ins. (6 cm)
8 sts wide

Begin here

Back of Head:

Begin with ch 3 (includes one for turning ch).

Row 1: Starting with the second chain from the hook, sc 2, ch 1.

Row 2: sc 2, ch 1.

Row 3: (sc inc) twice, ch 1.

Row 4: sc 4, ch 1.

Row 5: sc inc, sc 2, sc inc, ch 1.

Row 6: sc 6, ch 1.

Row 7: sc inc, sc 4, sc inc, ch 1.

Rows 8–16: sc 8, ch 1.

Row 17: sc2tog, sc 4, sc2tog, ch 1.

Row 18: sc2tog, sc 2, sc2tog, ch 1.

Row 19: sc 2, sc2tog, ch 1.

Row 20: sc 1, sc2tog, ch 1.

Row 21: sc2tog. Cut the yarn, leaving an 8-in. tail, then pull yarn through.

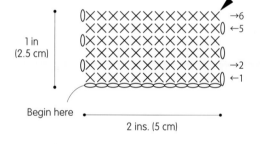

1 in
(2.5 cm)

Begin here

2 ins. (5 cm)

Upper Arms (make two):

Using crochet-in-the-round method, make center ring.

Round 1: ch 1, sc 6, ch 1. Begin each following round by crocheting into first stitch of previous round. Mark first stitch with a locking stitch marker to indicate the beginning of your rounds.

Round 2: (sc 1, sc inc) three times.

Rounds 3–7: sc 9.

Round 8: (sc 1, sc2tog) three times.

Round 9: sc 6. Cut the yarn, leaving an 8-in. tail, then pull yarn through.

Bow Tie:

Using D hook with medium-weight black yarn, ch 13 (includes one for tch).

Rows 1–6: sc 12, ch 1.

Cut the yarn, leaving a 6-in. tail, then pull yarn through. Weave in ends. Fold piece like an accordion, and tie in the middle with a scrap piece of black yarn to finish. Leave tails of scrap yarn to attach to bear later.

Whipstitch ear

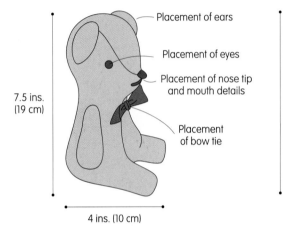

Placement of ears

Placement of eyes

Placement of nose tip
and mouth details

Placement
of bow tie

7.5 ins.
(19 cm)

4 ins. (10 cm)

Sew the Pieces Together:

Use the instructions on page 32 for how to assemble figures. Use the charts throughout the pattern for reference and piece placement. Use a little bit of toy stuffing in the arms and attach to bear. Use the whipstitch to attach ears to top of head. Use whipstitch to attach nose tip and embroider straight stitches to create mouth.

Accessorize:

For groom, attach bow tie to neck. For bride, make six small roses and one leaf (see following page for pattern). Attach three roses to top of head between the ears. Bundle the other three together with the leaf to create a bouquet. Attach bouquet between arms. Add a piece of lace or tulle to the top of head to create a veil.

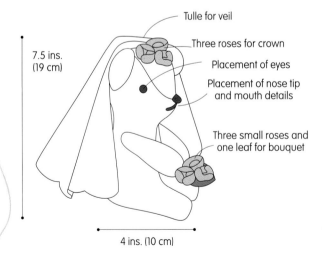

Tulle for veil

Three roses for crown

Placement of eyes

Placement of nose tip
and mouth details

Three small roses and
one leaf for bouquet

7.5 ins.
(19 cm)

4 ins. (10 cm)

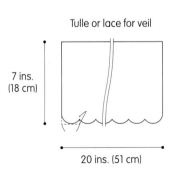

Tulle or lace for veil

7 ins.
(18 cm)

20 ins. (51 cm)

Roses

Materials:

- Roses: Medium-weight yarn (acrylic and wool blend) in red or pink, 9 yds (3g) for large blossoms, 6 yds (2g) for medium blossoms, 3 yds (1g) for small blossoms.
- Leaf: Medium-weight yarn (acrylic and wool blend) in green, 3 yds (1g).

Stitches Used:

Crochet: chain stitch (ch), single crochet (sc), half-double crochet (hdc), double crochet (dc) and slip stitch (sl st) Piecing: whipstitch. (See pages 10–13 for detailed stitch instructions.)

Tools:

- US size G/6 (4.25 mm) crochet hook
- Tapestry or yarn needle

Measurements:

Finished piece, large rose (including 2 leaves): 2.75 x 2 ins. (7 x 5 cm) *Note that measurements are approximate and will vary due to tension and yarn choice.*

Pattern Notes:

This pattern is worked flat for both the flower and the leaf. The flower is then rolled up to create the look of the rose petals.

Flower:

Begin with ch 9 (small rose), ch 16 (medium rose), or ch 24 (large rose).

Row 1: Beginning with the fourth ch from hook, dc 2 in same ch. Dc 3 in each chain remaining.

Row 2: (sl st, hdc 1, dc 1, hdc 1) three times, (sl st, hdc 1, dc 3, hdc 1) once for small blossom, three times for medium and large blossoms, (sl st, hdc 1, dc 5, hdc 1) once for medium blossom, four times for large blossom. Cut yarn, leaving an 8-in. tail, and pull through.

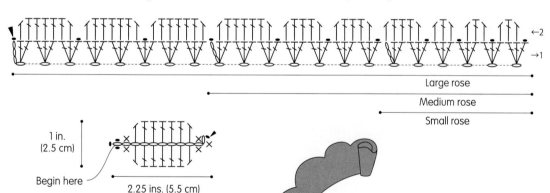

Leaf:

Using green yarn, begin with ch 11.

Row 1: Starting with second chain from hook, sc 1, hdc 1, dc 5, hdc 1, sc 1, sl st 3. Turn and continue down other side of starting chain. Sc 1, hdc 1, dc 5, hdc 1, sc 2, sl st. Cut yarn, leaving a 6-in. tail, and pull through.

Sew the Pieces Together:

To create the rose, roll the piece up from the starting point. When rolled, sew the bottom to hold flower together. Add leaf if desired and affix with whipstitch.

Raccoon

Materials:

- Bulky-weight yarn (acrylic and wool blend) in mustard or tan, 65 yds (40g)
- Bulky-weight yarn (acrylic and wool blend) in white and gray, 9 yds (5g) each
- Bulky-weight yarn (acrylic and wool blend) in dark gray, small amount of for nose and mouth details

Tools:

- US size H/8 (5.0mm) crochet hook
- Tapestry or yarn needle
- Locking stitch marker
- Sewing needle and cotton thread (if using buttons for eyes)
- Toy stuffing, 30g
- Two black buttons or safety animal eyes (9mm)

Measurements:

Finished piece is 6.75 x 6.75 x 4 ins. (17 x 17 x 10 cm)

Note that measurements are approximate and will vary due to tension and yarn choice.

Stitches Used:

Crochet: chain stitch (ch), turning chain (tch), single crochet (sc), single crochet increase (sc inc), single crochet decrease (sc2tog), slip stitch (sl st). Piecing and details: whipstitch and embroidery. (See pages 10–13 for detailed crochet stitch instructions.)

Pattern Notes:

This pattern is worked flat, back and forth in single crochet, creating four main body pieces and four detailing pieces. Arms and tail are crocheted in the round separately from the main body pieces. It is then assembled afterwards with yarn and a tapestry needle using the whipstitch.

Note: a ch 1 is at the end of every row. This is for the turning chain (tch), which is needed to begin the next row. The chart shows this at the beginning of each row.

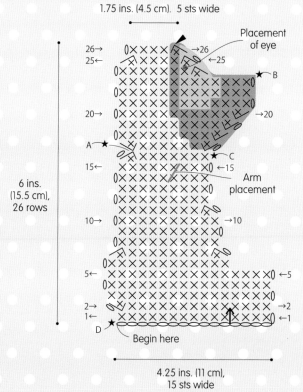

1.75 ins. (4.5 cm). 5 sts wide

Placement of eye

→26 ←25 B

→20

A C

←15

Arm placement

→10

←5

→2 ←1

D

Begin here

6 ins. (15.5 cm), 26 rows

4.25 ins. (11 cm), 15 sts wide

◁ Pass new yarn
◀ Break yarn
× Mustard
⊗ White
× Dark gray

Main Body, Head, Upper and Lower Legs (make two):

Using mustard yarn, begin with ch 16 (includes one for tch).

Row 1: Begin with second chain from hook, sc 14, ch 1.

Row 2: sc inc, sc 14, ch 1.

Rows 3–5: sc 16, ch 1.

Row 6: sc 12, ch 1, turn before reaching end of piece.

Row 7: sc2tog, sc 8, sc2tog, ch 1.

Rows 8–10: sc 10, ch 1.

Row 11: sc2tog, sc 8, ch 1.

Rows 12–15: sc 9, ch 1.

Row 16: sc2tog, sc 7, switch to white and ch 1.

Row 17: sc inc, sc 1, switch to mustard and sc 5, sc inc, ch 1.

Row 18: sc 6, switch to white and sc 3, sc inc, ch 1.

Row 19: sc inc, sc 4, switch to mustard) sc 6, ch 1.

Row 20: sc 5, switch to white and sc 6, sc inc, ch 1.

Row 21: sc 4, switch to gray and sc 3, switch to white and sc 1, switch to mustard) sc 5, ch 1.

Row 22: sc 5, switch to white and sc 1, switch to gray and sc 4, switch to white and sc 3, ch 1.

Row 23: sc 3, switch to gray and sc 4, switch to white and sc 1, switch to mustard and sc 5, ch 1.

Row 24: sc 5, switch to white and sc 1, switch to gray and sc 1, sc2tog, ch 1, turn before reaching end of piece.

Row 25: sc2tog, switch to white and sc 1, switch to mustard and sc 3, sc2tog, ch 1.

Row 26: sc 4, switch to white and sc2tog. Cut yarn, leaving a 6-in. tail, and pull through.

> Changing colors in a piece can be tricky. Be sure to keep all the working yarn and any ends on the same side so they can all be hidden on the inside once pieced together!

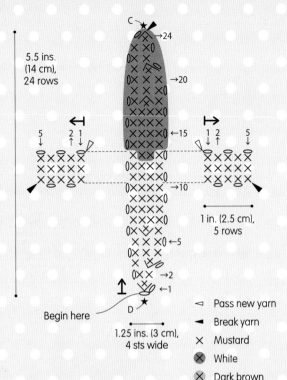

5.5 ins. (14 cm), 24 rows

C →24

→20

←15

5 ↓   2 ↑ 1   1 2 ↑ ↑   5 ↓

→10

1 in. (2.5 cm), 5 rows

←5

→2
←1

Begin here

D ★

1.25 ins. (3 cm), 4 sts wide

◁ Pass new yarn
◀ Break yarn
✕ Mustard
⊗ White
✖ Dark brown

Ears (make two):

Using mustard yarn and the crochet-in-the-round method (see detailed instructions on page 14), make a center ring.

Round 1: ch 1, sc 6, ch 1. Do not join with sl st. Turn and work back and forth to create the ear shape.

Round 2: sc 1, sc inc, sc 2, sc inc, sc 1. Cut the yarn, leaving an 8-in. tail, then pull yarn through.

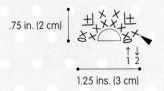

.75 in. (2 cm)

1 2

1.25 ins. (3 cm)

Underbody and Inner Legs:

Using mustard yarn, begin with ch 2 (one starting ch and one turning ch).

Row 1: Starting with the second chain from the hook, sc inc, ch 1.

Row 2: sc 2, ch 1.

Row 3: sc inc, sc 2, ch 1.

Rows 4–5: sc 3, ch 1.

Row 6: sc 1 sc inc, sc 1, ch 1.

Rows 7–12: sc 4, ch 1.

Row 13: sc 1, switch to white and sc 2, switch to mustard and sc 1, switch to white and ch 1.

Rows 14–17: sc 4, ch 1.

Row 18: sc 1 sc2tog, sc 1, ch 1.

Rows 19–20: sc 3, ch 1.

Row 21: sc2tog, sc 1, ch 1.

Rows 22–23: sc 2, ch 1.

Row 24: sc2tog. Cut the yarn, leaving a 6-in. tail, then pull yarn through.

Begin inner legs. Reattach mustard yarn at the thirteenth row of belly for first leg.

Row 1: ch 1, sc 3 across side, ch 1.

Rows 2–5: sc 3, ch 1. At the end of row 5, cut the yarn, leaving an 8-in. tail, then pull yarn through.

Repeat these rows on opposite side of belly for second leg.

> Be sure to leave a long tail here to use for embroidering face details.

Nose Tip:

Using dark gray yarn, ch 2.

Row 1: sc inc. Cut the yarn leaving an 8-in. tail, then pull yarn through.

Upper Arms (make two):

Using mustard yarn and the crochet-in-the-round method, make a center ring.

Round 1: ch 1, sc 5, ch 1. Begin each following round by crocheting into first stitch of previous round. Mark first stitch with a locking stitch marker to indicate the beginning of your rounds.

Round 2: (sc 1, sc inc) twice, sc 1.

Rounds 3–7: sc 8.

Round 8: (sc 1, sc2tog) twice, sc 1.

Round 9: sc 5. Cut the yarn, leaving an 8-in. tail, then pull yarn through.

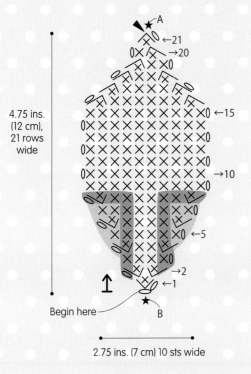

4.75 ins. (12 cm), 21 rows wide

Begin here

2.75 ins. (7 cm) 10 sts wide

Back of Head:

Using mustard yarn, begin with ch 2 (includes one for turning ch).

Row 1: Starting with the second chain from the hook, sc inc, ch 1.

Row 2: (sc inc) twice, switch to white and ch 1.

Row 3: sc 1, switch to mustard and sc 2, switch to white and sc 1, ch 1.

Row 4: sc inc, switch to mustard and sc 2, switch to white and sc inc, switch to gray and ch 1.

Row 5: sc 1, switch to white and sc 1, switch to mustard sc 2, switch to white sc 1, switch to gray and sc 1, ch 1.

Row 6: sc inc, switch to white and sc 1, switch to mustard and sc 2, and switch to white and sc 1, switch to gray and sc inc, ch 1.

Row 7: sc 2, switch to white and sc 1, switch to mustard and sc 2, switch to white and sc 1, switch to gray and sc 2, switch to white and ch 1.

Row 8: sc inc, sc 2, switch to mustard and sc 2, switch to white and sc 2, sc inc, switch to mustard and ch 1.

Rows 9–15: sc 10, ch 1.

Row 16: sc2tog, sc 6, sc2tog, ch 1.

Row 17: sc2tog, sc 4, sc2tog, ch 1

Row 18: sc2tog, sc 2, sc2tog, ch 1.

Row 19: sc 2, sc2tog, ch 1.

Row 20: sc 1, sc2tog, ch 1.

Row 21: sc2tog. Cut the yarn, leaving an 8-in. tail, then pull yarn through.

Tail:

Using gray yarn and the crochet-in-the-round method, make a center ring.

Round 1: ch 1, sc 6, sl st.

Round 2: ch 1, (sc inc) six times, sl st.

Round 3: ch 1, sc 12, sl st. Switch to mustard yarn.

Rounds 4 & 5: ch 1, sc 12, sl st. Switch to gray yarn.

Rounds 6 & 7: ch 1, sc 12, sl st. Switch to mustard yarn.

Rounds 8 & 9: ch 1, sc 12, sl st. Switch to gray yarn.

Round 10: ch 1, (sc 2, sc2tog) three times, sl st.

Round 11: ch 1, sc 9, sl st. Switch to mustard yarn.

Rounds 12 & 13: ch 1, sc 9, sl st. Cut the yarn, leaving an 8-in. tail, then pull yarn through.

Raccoon

Sew the Pieces Together:

Refer to the instructions on pages 16 and 32 for how to assemble figures. Use the charts throughout the pattern for reference and piece placement.

When attaching back of head to main body piece, take care to line up the colors and use the corresponding color yarn in your stitches. Use a little bit of toy stuffing in the arms and attach to raccoon. Use the whipstitch to attach ears to top of head. Use whipstitch to attach nose tip and embroider straight stitches to create mouth. Stuff the tip of the tail, then flatten the end. When sewing the tail to body, be sure to place the seam side down.

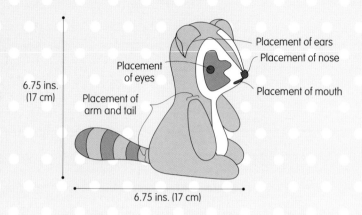

6.75 ins. (17 cm)

6.75 ins. (17 cm)

Placement of ears

Placement of nose

Placement of eyes

Placement of mouth

Placement of arm and tail

Apples & Pears

Materials:

- Apple: Medium-weight yarn (acrylic and wool blend) in red or lime, 17 yds (7g)
- Pear: Medium-weight yarn (acrylic and wool blend) in green or yellow, 28 yds (12g)
- Stems (both): Medium-weight yarn (acrylic and wool blend) in dark brown 3 yds (1g)

Tools:

- US size G/6 (4.25 mm) crochet hook
- Tapestry or yarn needle
- Toy stuffing, small amount
- Locking stitch marker

Stitches Used:

Chain stitch (ch), single crochet (sc), single crochet increase (sc inc), single crochet decrease (sc2tog), slip stitch (sl st) and whipstitch. (See pages 10–13 for detailed instructions.)

Measurements:

Finished pieces are 2 x 2 ins. (5 x 5 cm—apple); 2.25 x 3.75 ins. (5.5 x 9.5 cm—pear)

*Note that measurements are approximate and will vary due to tension and yarn choice.

Pattern Notes:

This pattern is worked in the round for both the apple and pear.

Apple

Using red or lime yarn and the crochet-in-the-round method, make a center ring. (See page 14 for detailed instructions.)

Round 1: ch 1, sc 8. Begin each following round by crocheting into first stitch of previous round. Mark first stitch of each new round with a locking stitch marker.

Round 2: (sc inc) 8 times.

Rounds 3–4: sc 16.

Round 5: (sc 1, sc inc) 8 times.

Rounds 6–7: sc 24.

Round 8: (sc inc, sc 5) 4 times.

Round 9–10: sc 28.

Round 11: sc 4, (sc inc, sc 6) 3 times, sc 2.

Rounds 12–14: sc 32.

Round 15: (sc2tog, sc 3) 6 times, sc2tog. Stuff with toy stuffing about 80% of the way now, before beginning next decrease round.

Round 16: (sc 2, sc2tog) 6 times, sc 1.

Round 17: (sc2tog) 9 times, sc 1, sl st. Cut yarn, leaving an 8-in. tail, and pull through.

Stem (for both):

Using brown yarn, begin with ch 7.

Row 1: Starting with second chain from hook, sc 6. Cut yarn, leaving an 8-in. tail, and pull through.

Fold stem in half lengthwise. Sew together with the whipstitch, using the tail.

Pear

Using green or yellow yarn and the crochet-in-the-round method, make a center ring. (See page 14 for detailed instructions.)

Round 1: ch 1, sc 8. Begin each following round by crocheting into first stitch of previous round. Mark first stitch of each new round with a locking stitch marker.

Round 3: (sc 1, sc inc) 8 times.

Round 4: sc 24.

Round 5: (sc 2, sc inc) 8 times.

Rounds 6–11: sc 32.

Round 12: (sc2tog , sc 2) 8 times.

Round 13: sc 24.

Round 14: (sc 2, sc2tog) 6 times.

Rounds 15-18: sc 18. Stuff with toy stuffing about 80% of the way now, before beginning next decrease round.

Round 19: (sc 1, sc2tog) six times.

Round 20: (sc2tog) six times, sl st. Cut yarn, leaving an 8-in. tail, and pull through.

Fill the top with more stuffing to the desired firmness.

Finishing Details:

For both, insert stem into top and sew closed.

When finishing the apple, use the remaining tail to weave through the bottom and back through the top to create the dimples. Fasten off yarn and weave in ends.

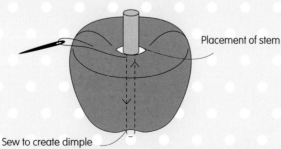

Placement of stem

Sew to create dimple

Tweet Street

Stitches Used:

Crochet: chain stitch (ch), single crochet (sc), single crochet increase (sc inc), single crochet decrease (sc2tog), half-double crochet (hdc), double crochet (dc) and slip stitch (sl st). Piecing and details: whipstitch. (See pages 10–13 for detailed stitch instructions.)

Materials:

- Medium-weight yarn (acrylic and wool blend) in white, 25 yds (10 g)
- Medium-weight yarn (acrylic and wool blend) in color of your choice for wings/tail, 7 yds (3g)
- Medium-weight yarn (acrylic and wool blend) in yellow, 5 yds (2g)

Tools:

- US size G/6 (4.25 mm) crochet hook
- Tapestry or yarn needle
- Small amount of toy stuffing
- Locking stitch marker
- Black buttons or safety animal eyes (6 mm)

Measurements:

Finished piece: 4 x 3.25 ins. (10 x 7 cm)

*Note that measurements are approximate and *will* vary due to tension and yarn choice.

Pattern Notes:

This pattern is worked in the round for the main body and head, with six flat detailing pieces attached at the end.

Main Body:

Using the white yarn and the crochet-in-the-round method, make a center ring. (See page 14 for detailed instructions)

Round 1: ch 1, sc 6. Begin each following round by crocheting into first stitch of previous round. Mark first stitch with a locking stitch marker to indicate the beginning of your rounds.

Round 2: (sc inc) six times.

Round 3: (sc 3, sc inc) three times.

Rounds 4–8: sc 15.

Round 9: sc 5, sc2tog, sc 1, sc2tog, sc 5.

Round 10: sc 3, sc2tog, sc 2, sc2tog, sc 4.

Before completing the final two rounds, stuff with toy stuffing to desired fullness.

Round 11: sc 4, sc2tog, sc 5.

Round 12: (sc2tog) 5 times, sl st. Cut yarn, leaving an 8-in. tail, and pull through.

Head:

Using the white yarn and the crochet-in-the round method, make a center ring.

Round 1: ch 1, sc 6. Begin each following round by crocheting into first stitch of previous round. Mark first stitch with a locking stitch marker to indicate the beginning of your rounds.

Round 2: (sc inc) six times.

Round 3: (sc inc, sc 1) six times.

Rounds 4–7: sc 18.

Round 8: (sc 1, sc2tog) six times. Before completing the final round, place safety eyes (consult diagram for placement) and stuff with toy stuffing to desired fullness.

Round 9: (sc2tog) six times, sl st. Cut yarn, leaving an 8-in. tail, and pull through.

Feet (make two):

Using the yellow yarn, ch 3.

Row 1: Beginning in second chain from hook, sc 2. Cut yarn, leaving a 6-in. tail and pull through.

Beak:

Using the yellow yarn, ch 5.

Row 1: Starting with second chain from hook, sc 4. Cut yarn, leaving a 6-in. tail, and pull through.

Tail:

Using the contrasting color, ch 11.

Row 1: Beginning in fifth ch from hook, dc 2, hdc 3, sc 2. Cut yarn, leaving a 6-in. tail, and pull through.

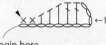

Begin here

Wings (make two):

Using the contrasting color, ch 8.

Row 1: Beginning in second ch from hook, sc 1, hdc 1, dc 3, hdc 1, sc 1. Cut yarn, leaving a 6-in. tail, and pull through.

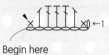

Begin here

Sew the Pieces Together:

Using the whipstitch, attach head to body (consult the diagrams and photos for placement). Insert end of tail into back of body and sew closed. Place wings on sides of body and use the whipstitch to sew halfway across the top and bottom. Leave the back of wings free. Fold beak in half and attach to the front of the face. Sew the two feet to the bottom.

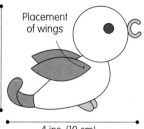

Placement of wings

3.25 ins. (7 cm)

4 ins. (10 cm)

Make the wings and body in different colors to make each bird one of a kind. You can also place the wings at different angles to give them each their own personality!

Simply Adorable Crochet

Quacker Family

Materials:

Mama Quacker—

- Medium-weight yarn (acrylic and wool blend) in white, 80 yds (50g)
- Medium-weight yarn (acrylic and wool blend) in orange, 12 yds (5g)
- Medium-weight yarn (acrylic and wool blend) in yellow, 10 yds (4g)

Baby Quackers (per duckling)—

- Medium-weight yarn (acrylic and wool blend) in yellow, 55 yds (23g)
- Medium-weight yarn (acrylic and wool blend) in orange, 16 yds (7g)

Tools:

- US size G/6 (4.25mm) crochet hook
- Tapestry or yarn needle
- Sewing needle and cotton thread (If using buttons for eyes)
- Toy stuffing, 30g for Mama Quacker, 15g for ducklings
- Two black buttons or safety animal eyes (9mm) for each duck.

Measurements:

Mama Quacker—7 x 6.25 x 3.5 ins. (19 x 16 x 9 cm)

Baby Quackers—4.25 x 3.5 x 2 ins. (11 x 9 x 5 cm) each

Note that measurements are approximate and will vary due to tension and yarn choice.

Stitches Used:

Crochet: chain stitch (ch), turning chain (tch), single crochet (sc), single crochet increase (sc inc), single crochet decrease (sc2tog), Slip Stitch (sl st). Piecing and details: whipstitch and embroidery. (See pages 10–13 for detailed stitch instructions.)

Special stitch used for this figure—single crochet triple Increase (sc3inc): single crochet three times into the same stitch.

Note: a ch 1 is at the end of every row. This is for the turning chain (tch), which is needed to begin the next row. The chart shows this at the beginning of each row.

Pattern Notes:

This pattern is worked flat, back and forth in single crochet, creating two main body pieces and six detailing pieces. It is then assembled afterwards with yarn and a tapestry needle using the whipstitch.

Mama Quacker

Main Body and Head (make two):

Using white yarn, begin with ch 11 (includes one for tch).

Row 1: Begin with second chain from hook, sc 10, ch 1.

Row 2: sc inc, sc 8, sc inc, ch 1.

Row 3: sc inc, sc 10, sc inc, ch 1.

Row 4: sc inc, sc 12, sc inc, ch 1.

Row 5: sc inc, sc 14, sc inc, ch 1.

Row 6: sc inc, sc 16, sc inc, ch 1.

Row 7: sc inc, sc 19, ch 1.

Row 8: sc 20, sc inc, ch 1.

Rows 9–10: sc 22, ch 1.

Row 11: sc 3, sc2tog, ch 1. Turn before reaching end of piece.

Row 12: sc2tog, sc 2, ch 1.

Row 13: sc 1, sc2tog, ch 1.

Row 14: sc2tog. Cut yarn, leaving a 6-in. tail, and pull through.

Reattach yarn where row 11 ended. Ch 1.

Row 11 (continued): sc2tog, sc 13, sc2tog, ch 1.

Row 12: sc 12, sc2tog, ch 1.

Row 13: sc2tog, sc 10, ch 1.

Row 14: sc 8, sc2tog, ch 1.

Row 15: sc2tog, sc 7, ch 1.

Continue with neck:

Row 1: sc2tog, sc 6, ch 1.

Rows 2–8: sc 7, ch 1. At the end of row 8, ch 3 to begin the head.

Continue with head:

Row 1: Begin with second chain from hook, sc 9, ch 1.

Row 2: sc inc, sc 7, sc inc, ch 1.

Row 3: sc 11, sc inc, ch 1.

Row 4: sc inc, sc 10, ch 1.

Row 5: sc inc, sc 11, ch 1.

Rows 6–7: sc 13, ch 1.

Row 8: sc 11, sc2tog, ch 1.

Row 9: sc 10, sc2tog, ch 1.

Row 10: sc2tog, sc 7, sc2tog, ch 1.

Row 11: sc 3, sc2tog, sc 2, sc2tog, ch 1.

Row 12: sc2tog, sc 3, sc2tog. Cut yarn, leaving a 6-in. tail, and pull through.

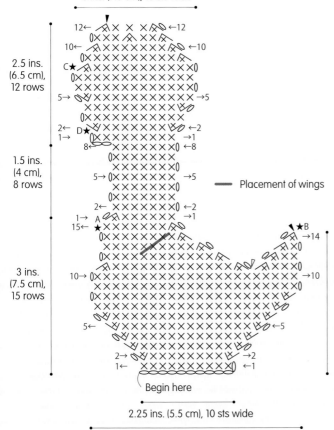

3 ins. (7.5 cm), 13 sts wide

2.5 ins. (6.5 cm), 12 rows

1.5 ins. (4 cm), 8 rows

— Placement of wings

3 ins. (7.5 cm), 15 rows

Begin here

2.25 ins. (5.5 cm), 10 sts wide

5.25 ins (13.5 cm), 22 sts wide

Underbody:

Using white yarn, begin with ch 2 (one starting ch and one turning ch).

Row 1: Starting with the second chain from the hook, sc 1, ch 1.

Row 2: sc inc, ch 1.

Rows 3 & 4: sc 2, ch 1.

Row 5: sc 1, sc inc, ch 1.

Rows 6–7: sc 3, ch 1.

Row 8: sc 2, sc inc, ch 1.

Row 9: sc 4, ch 1.

Row 10: sc inc, sc 3, ch 1.

Row 11: sc 5, ch 1.

Row 12: sc 4, sc inc, ch 1.

Row 13: sc 5, sc inc, ch 1.

Row 14: sc 7, ch 1.

Row 15: sc inc, sc 6, ch 1.

Row 16: sc inc, sc 7, ch 1.

Row 17: sc 9, ch 1.

Row 18: sc 8, sc inc, ch 1.

Row 19: sc 9, sc inc, ch 1.

Row 20: sc 11, ch 1.

Row 21: sc inc, sc 10, ch 1.

Row 22: sc inc, sc 11, ch 1.

Rows 23–27: sc 13, ch 1.

Row 28: sc2tog, sc 9, sc2tog, ch 1.

Row 29: sc 11, ch 1.

Row 30: sc2tog, sc 7, sc2tog, ch 1.

Row 31: sc 9, ch 1.

Row 32: sc2tog, sc 5, sc2tog, ch 1.

Row 33: sc 3, sc2tog, sc 2, ch 1.

Row 34: sc2tog, sc 2, sc2tog, ch 1.

Rows 35–37: sc 4, ch 1.

Row 38: (sc2tog) twice, ch 1.

Row 39: sc2tog, ch 1.

Row 40: sc 1. Cut the yarn, leaving a 6-in. tail, then pull yarn through.

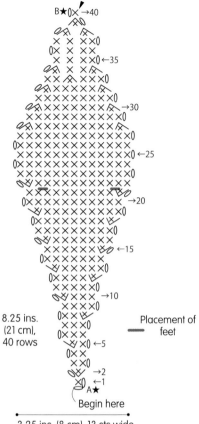

8.25 ins. (21 cm), 40 rows

Placement of feet

3.25 ins. (8 cm), 13 sts wide

Feet (make four):

Using orange yarn, begin with ch 2 (includes one for turning ch).

Row 1: Starting with the second chain from the hook, sc inc, ch 1.

Row 2: (sc inc) twice, ch 1.

Row 3: sc 4, ch 1.

Row 4: sc inc, sc 2, sc inc, ch 1.

Row 5: sc 6, ch 1.

Row 6: sc inc, sc 4, sc inc. Cut the yarn, leaving a 6-in. tail, then pull yarn through.

Row 7: Reattach yarn in third stitch, sl st, sc 2, sl st, ch 1.

Row 8: sc2tog. Cut the yarn, leaving an 8-in. tail, then pull yarn through.

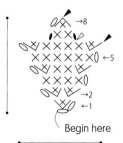

2 ins. (5 cm)

Begin here

1.5 ins. (4 cm), 8 sts wide

Wings (make two):

Using white yarn, begin with ch 2 (includes one for turning ch).

Row 1: Starting with the second chain from the hook, sc3inc, ch 1.

Row 2: sc inc, sc 1, sc inc, ch 1.

Row 3: sc 5, ch 1.

Row 4: sc 4, sc inc, ch 1.

Row 5: sc 6, ch 1.

Row 6: sc 5, sc inc, ch 1.

Rows 7–9: sc 7, ch 1.

Row 10: sc2tog, sc 5, ch 1.

Row 11: sc2tog, sc 4, ch 1.

Row 12: sc 5, ch 1.

Row 13: sc2tog, sc 3, ch 1.

Row 14: sc 2, sc2tog, ch 1.

Row 15: sc2tog, sc 1, ch 1.

Row 16: sc2tog. Cut the yarn, leaving a 6-in. tail, then pull yarn through.

3.5 ins. (9 cm), 16 rows

→16
←15
→10
←5
→2
←1
A★
Begin here

1.75 ins. (4.5 cm), 7 sts wide

Upper Beak:

Using yellow yarn and the crochet-in-the-round method (see page 14 for detailed instructions), make a center ring.

Round 1: ch 1, sc 6, sl st, ch 1. Mark first stitch with a locking stitch marker to indicate the beginning of your rounds.

Round 2: (sc inc) six times, sl st, ch 1.

Round 3: sc 12, sl st, ch 1.

Round 4: (sc 3, sc2tog) twice, sc 3, sl st, ch 1.

Round 5: sc 10, sl st, ch 1.

Round 6: sc 3, (sc2tog) twice, sc 3, sl st, ch 1.

Round 7: sc 8. Cut the yarn, leaving an 8-in. tail, then pull yarn through.

Lower Beak:

Using yellow yarn, begin with ch 3.

Row 1: Starting with the second chain from the hook, sc 2, sc3inc. Continue down other side of starting chain. Sc 2, sc inc 3, sl st, ch 1.

Row 2: sc 3, sc3inc, sc 3, sl st. Cut the yarn, leaving an 8-in. tail, then pull yarn through.

1 in. (2.5 cm)

Begin here

1.25 ins. (3.5 cm)

Baby Quacker

Main Body and Head (make two):

Using yellow yarn, begin with ch 6 (includes one for tch).

Row 1: Begin with second chain from hook, sc 5, ch 1.

Row 2: sc inc, sc 3, sc inc, ch 1.

Row 3: sc inc, sc 5, sc inc, ch 1.

Row 4: sc inc, sc 7, sc inc, ch 1.

Row 5: sc inc, sc 10, ch 1.

Row 6: sc 12, ch 1.

Row 7: sc 10, sc2tog, ch 1.

Row 8: sc 11, ch 1.

Row 9: sc 2, sc2tog, ch 1. Turn before reaching end of piece.

Row 10: sc2tog, sc 1, ch 1.

Row 11: sc2tog. Cut yarn, leaving a 6-in. tail, and pull through.

Reattach yarn where row 9 ended. Ch 1.

Row 9 (continued): sc2tog, sc 3, sc2tog, ch 2.

Continue with head:

Row 1: Begin with second chain from hook, sc 4, sc inc, ch 1.

Row 2: sc inc, sc 4, sc inc, ch 1.

Row 3: sc 7, sc inc, ch 1.

Row 4: sc 9, ch 1.

Row 5: sc inc, sc 8, ch 1.

Rows 6–7: sc 10, ch 1.

Row 8: sc 8, sc2tog, ch 1.

Row 9: sc 9, ch 1.

Row 10: sc2tog, sc 1, sc2tog, sc 4, ch 1.

Row 11: sc 7, ch 1.

Row 12: sc2tog, sc 3, sc2tog. Cut yarn leaving a 6-in. tail and pull through.

2.25 ins. (6 cm)
10 sts wide

2.5 ins. (6.5 cm)
12 Rows

2 ins. (5 cm)
9 Rows

2.5 ins. (6 cm),
11 rows

Begin here

1.25 ins. (3 cm),
5 sts wide

Wings (make two):

Begin with ch 2 (includes one for turning ch).

Row 1: Starting with the second chain from the hook, sc3inc, ch 1.

Row 2: sc inc, sc 1, sc inc, ch 1.

Rows 3–4: sc 5, ch 1.

Row 5: sc 3, sc2tog, ch 1.

Row 6: sc2tog, sc 2, ch 1.

Row 7: sc 1, sc2tog, ch 1.

Row 8: sc2tog. Cut the yarn, leaving a 6-in. tail, then pull yarn through.

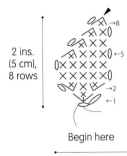

2 ins.
(5 cm),
8 rows

Begin here

1.25 ins. (3 cm),
5 sts wide

Underbody:

Begin with ch 2 (one starting ch and one turning ch).

Row 1: Starting with the second chain from the hook, sc 1, ch 1.

Row 2: sc inc, ch 1.

Rows 3–4: sc 2, ch 1.

Row 5: sc 1, sc inc, ch 1.

Rows 6–7: sc 3, ch 1.

Row 8: sc 2, sc inc, ch 1.

Row 9: sc 4, ch 1.

Row 10: sc inc, sc 3, ch 1.

Row 11: sc inc, sc 4, ch 1.

Row 12: sc 6, ch 1.

Row 13: sc 5, sc inc, ch 1.

Row 14: sc 6, sc inc, ch 1.

Rows 15–16: sc 8, ch 1.

Row 17: sc2tog, sc 4, sc2tog, ch 1.

Row 18: sc 6, ch 1.

Row 19: sc2tog, sc 2, sc2tog, ch 1.

Row 20: sc 4, ch 1.

Row 21: (sc2tog) twice, ch 1.

Rows 22–24: sc 2, ch 1.

Row 25: sc2tog, ch 1.

Row 26: sc 1. Cut the yarn, leaving a 6-in. tail, then pull yarn through.

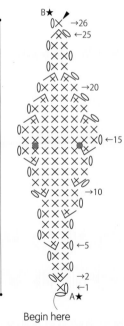

2.5 in.
(6.5 cm)
12 rows

Begin here

● Placement of feet

Simply Adorable Crochet

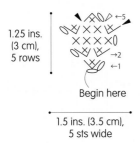

1.25 ins.
(3 cm),
5 rows

Begin here

1.5 ins. (3.5 cm),
5 sts wide

Feet (make four):

Using orange yarn, begin with ch 2 (includes one for turning ch).

Row 1: Starting with the second chain from the hook, sc inc, ch 1.

Row 2: (sc inc) twice, ch 1.

Row 3: sc 4, ch 1.

Row 4: sc inc, sc 2, sc inc, ch 1. Cut the yarn, leaving a 6-in. tail, then pull yarn through.

Row 5: Reattach yarn in third stitch, ch 1, sc2tog. Cut the yarn, leaving an 8-in. tail, then pull yarn through.

Upper Beak:

Using orange yarn and the crochet-in-the-round method, make a center ring.

Round 1: ch 1, sc 5, sl st, ch 1. Mark first stitch with a locking stitch marker to indicate the beginning of your rounds.

Round 2: (sc inc) five times, sl st, ch 1.

Round 3: sc 10, sl st, ch 1.

Round 4: sc 3, (sc2tog) twice, sc 3, sl st, ch 1.

Round 5: sc 8. Cut the yarn, leaving an 8-in. tail, then pull yarn through.

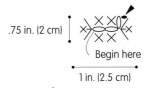

.75 in. (2 cm)

Begin here

1 in. (2.5 cm)

Lower Beak:

Using orange yarn, begin with ch 3.

Row 1: Starting with the second chain from the hook, sc 2, sc3inc. Continue down other side of starting chain. Sc 2, sc3inc, sl st. Cut the yarn, leaving an 8-in. tail, then pull yarn through.

Sew the Pieces Together:

Begin by matching up the star points on one side of duck and underbody. Using whipstitch, sew together from A to B. Place the other side of duck to the underbody and also attach from A to B.

Sew up neck from A to D, but leave D to C open. Sew up back of duck from B to C. Stuff with toy stuffing as you go. Stuff the neck of the mama duck firmly to support her head. Before attaching the beak, be sure to place your safety eyes (refer to photos for placement), then stuff the head.

Lightly stuff the upper beak, flatten, and sew shut. With the seam side down, attach the upper beak to the lower beak. Insert into opening left between C and D and use the whipstitch to attach.

Make the feet: use the whipstitch to sew the tops to the bottoms. Fill each lightly with toy stuffing before closing up completely. Sew to the bottom of the duck, using the chart for placement.

If desired, use the pattern on page 130 to make the clover accessories for your Quacker Family.

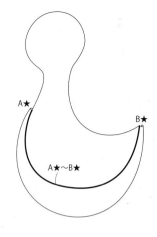

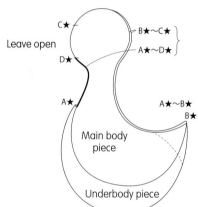

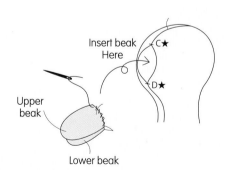

Simply Adorable Crochet

Butterflies

Materials:

- Medium-weight yarn (acrylic and wool blend) in yellow or blue, 6 yds (2g)
- Medium-weight yarn (acrylic and wool blend) in white, 3 yds (1g)

Tools:

- US size C/2 (2.5 mm) crochet hook
- Tapestry or yarn needle

Stitches Used:

Chain stitch (ch), double crochet (dc), double crochet cluster (dc CL), half-double crochet (hdc), single crochet (sc) and slip stitch (sl st). (See pages 10–13 for detailed stitch instructions.)

Special stitch used for this figure—Crochet around the chain Instead of crocheting into both loops of the chain, reach below the starting chain, go in the space between the stitches and grab the yarn to work the stitch.

Measurements:

Finished piece, 2.5 x 2 ins. (6 x 5 cm)

Note that measurements are approximate and will vary due to tension and yarn choice.

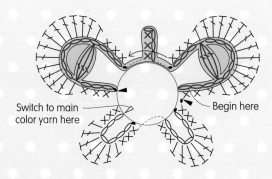

Switch to main color yarn here

Begin here

Body:

Using white yarn and the crochet-in-the-round method (see detailed instructions on page 14), make a center ring.

Round 1: ch 10, dc CL into fourth chain, ch 3, sl st into center ring. Ch 4, starting in second chain from hook, sc 3, sl st into center ring. Ch 10, dc CL into fourth chain, ch 3, sl st into center ring. Cut yarn, leaving a 6-in. tail, and pull through.

Using yellow or blue yarn, reattach yarn to center ring with ch 1 (refer to the chart for placment). Ch 6 more, then sl st into center ring. Ch 1 in center ring, then ch 6 more. Sl st into center ring. Pull tail of center ring to close loop.

Round 2: Crocheting around the chain, begin round 2 with large right wing. Sc 3, hdc 1, dc 12, hdc 1, sc 3. Carry yarn over antenna, and repeat for large left wing.

Make first small wing: sc 3, hdc 1, dc 5, hdc 1, sc 3. Repeat sequence for second small wing. Cut yarn, leaving a 6-in. tail, and pull through.

Weave in ends to finish.

Mice

Materials:

- Medium-weight yarn (acrylic and wool blend) in white or gray, 25 yds (10 g)

Tools:

- US size G/6 (4.25 mm) crochet hook
- Tapestry or yarn needle
- Small amount of toy stuffing
- Locking stitch marker
- Black buttons or safety animal eyes (6 mm)

Pattern Notes:

his pattern is worked in the round for the nain body, with three flat detailing pieces attached at the end.

Stitches Used:

Crochet: chain stitch (ch), single crochet (sc), single crochet increase (sc inc), single crochet decrease (sc2tog) and slip stitch (sl st). Piecing and details: whipstitch. (See pages 10–13 for detailed instructions.)

Measurements:

Finished piece: 1.5 x 3 ins. (4 x 7.5 cm)

Note that measurements are approximate and will vary due to tension and yarn choice.

Main Body:

Using the crochet-in-the-round method, make a center ring (see page 14 for detailed instructions).

Round 1: ch 1, sc 4, sl st. Mark first stitch with a locking stitch marker to indicate the beginning of your rounds.

Round 2: ch 1, (sc 1, sc inc) twice, sl st.

Round 3: ch 1, (sc inc, sc 1) three times, sl st.

Round 4: ch 1, sc 9, sl st.

Round 5: ch 1, (sc 2, sc inc) three times, sl st.

Round 6: ch 1, sc 12, sl st.

Round 7: ch 1, (sc 3, sc inc) three times, sl st.

Round 8: ch 1, sc 15, sl st.

Round 9: ch 1, (sc 4, sc inc) three times, sl st.

Rounds 10–11: ch 1, sc 18, sl st.

Round 12: ch 1, (sc 2, sc2tog) four times, sc 2, sl st.

Before completing the final two rounds, place safety eyes in desired location (use the diagrams for placement). Stuff body with toy stuffing to desired fullness.

Round 13: ch 1, (sc 1, sc2tog) four times, sc2tog, sl st.

Round 14: ch 1, (sc2tog) four times, sc 1, sl st. Cut yarn, leaving an 8-in. tail, and pull through.

Ears (make two):

Using the crochet-in-the-round method, make a center ring.

Row 1: ch 1, sc 7. Cut yarn, leaving an 8-in. tail, and pull through.

Repeat for second ear.

Tail:

Make a chain of 18 stitches. Cut the yarn, leaving a 12-in. tail minimum. To give the tail some curl, use the whipstitch around the chain.

Finishing Details:

Attach ears above the eyes using the whipstitch. Insert end of tail into final round of main body and stitch closed.

> Have a furry friend? Add some catnip to your toy stuffing to make a great toy for your cat!

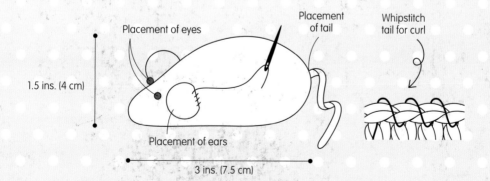

Placement of eyes

Placement of tail

Whipstitch tail for curl

1.5 ins. (4 cm)

Placement of ears

3 ins. (7.5 cm)

A görögök már az ókor-...égek gyógyítására. Latin ...zkes virágzatba tömörülő ...ulént tartalmaznak. Drogja ...bb házi orvosság. Forrá-...v-, torokgyulladás ese-...lgörcs ellen, szélhajtó ...ját tisztán vagy más ...éskor itatják. Az azu-...szerek nyugtatják a bőrfe-...kereskedelemben forgalmazott kamilladrog 60%-a ...ilágkereskedelemben forgalmazott kamilladrog 60%-a a magy...lföld szikes pusztáiról származik.

2. Cicka... (Achillea fajok). A cic... honos fajai
a kamill...k hasonlóan gyulladáscsö... ...gyületet tar-
talmazna... Sebgyógyító hatását hár... ...merik. Teája
a vese-...nájbetegségek gyógysze... ...ztő, ...ke
a gyomo...az epeműködést. Rend... ...k, idő
panaszok...rvossága is. Vérszegénység elleni, ...gtató
teák egyik...kotórésze. (L.: Vadvirágok 2., 40. o...)

3. Pozsgás...ázsa (Lepidium ...n). ...Alföld szikes
pusztáinak...legzetes, húsos ...ó ...aye. Gyógyító
hatását csa...z utóbbi idő... ... Igyuk
influenzajár...yok idején! Öblöge... ...ken ...k-...
gyulladás elle...is jó.

4. Szöszös ö...arkkóró (Verbascum phlomoid... ...ga gliko-
zidot, nyálká...zaponint tartalmaz. Gyógyhatá... ...ár Plinius is
ismerte. Teá...elsősorban légcsőhurut és bélh... ...t ellen adják.
Izzasztó, víz...hajtó hatásáért is isszák. A nép...gyászat tejes
főzetét tüd...sz ellen ajánlotta, olajos kivonata... fagyási sérü-
léseket, bőr...egségeket kezeltek. (L.: Vadvirág... ...., 48. o.)

18

Pretty Posies & Plants

Flower Basket

Materials:

- Bulky-weight yarn (acrylic and wool blend) in gray, 25 yds (15g)

Tools:

- US size H/8 (4.25 mm) crochet hook
- Tapestry or yarn needle
- Locking stitch marker

Measurements:

Finished piece, 4 x 2 ins. (10 x 5 cm)

Note that measurements are approximate and will vary due to tension and yarn choice.

Pattern Notes:

This pattern is worked in the round for the basket and flat for the handle. It is then assembled afterwards with yarn and a tapestry needle using the whipstitch.

Stitches Used:

Crochet: Chain stitch (ch), double crochet cluster (dc CL), single crochet (sc), single crochet increase (sc inc) and slip stitch (sl st). Piecing and details: whipstitch. (See pages 10–13 for detailed stitch instructions.)

Special stitch used for this figure—double crochet cluster increase (dc CL inc)—dc CL, ch 1, dc CL in same stitch.

Bowl of Basket:

Using the crochet-in-the-round method, make a center ring. (See page 14 for detailed stitch instructions.)

Round 1: ch 1, sc 7, sl st. Mark first stitch with a locking stitch marker to indicate the beginning of your rounds.

Round 2: ch 1, (sc inc) seven times, sl st.

Round 3: ch 1, (sc 1, sc inc) seven times, sl st.

Round 4: ch 1, sc 1, (sc inc, sc 2) six times, sc inc, sc 1, sl st.

Round 5: ch 1, (sc 3, sc inc) six times, sc 4, sl st.

Note for this round: Every time a ch 1 is made, skip a stitch in the previous row and work your dc CL in the next stitch.

Round 6: ch 3, dc 2 into first st of previous round, ch 1, dc CL in same stitch, ([ch 1, dc CL] three times, dc CL inc) three times, (ch 1, dc CL) four times, ch1, sl st.

Rounds 7–8: ch 3, dc 2 into first st of previous round, ch 1, (dc CL, ch 1) twenty times, sl st. Cut yarn, leaving an 8-in. tail, and pull through.

Handle:

Begin with ch 35.

Row 1: Starting with second chain from hook, sc 34, ch 1.

Row 2: sc 34. Cut yarn, leaving a long tail, and pull through.

Fold handle in half lengthwise and use the whipstitch to sew closed for stability.

Piecing:

Use the whipstitch to sew handle to basket.

Lily of the Valley

Materials:

- Medium-weight yarn (acrylic and wool blend) in white, light green and dark green, 6 yds each (2g)

Tools:

- US size C/2 (2.5 mm) crochet hook
- Tapestry or yarn needle

Stitches Used:

Crochet: chain stitch (ch), double crochet (dc), half-double crochet (hdc), single crochet (sc) and slip stitch (sl st). Piecing: whipstitch. (See pages 10–13 for detailed stitch instructions.)

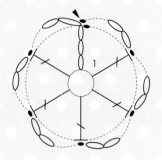

Flower (make three):

Using white yarn and the crochet-in-the-round method (see page 14 for detailed stitch instructions), make a center ring.

Round 1: ch 3, dc 5, sl st. Pull tail of center ring to close loop.

Round 2: (ch 2, sl st) six times. Cut yarn, leaving a 6-in. tail, and pull through.

Stem:

Using light green yarn, ch 26.

Row 1: Beginning with second chain from hook, sl st 5. Ch 3, work sl st in second chain from hook, sl st 6 down new chain and continue back down starting chain. Ch 5, work sl st in second chain from hook, sl st 18 down new chain and finish down starting chain. Cut yarn and pull through.

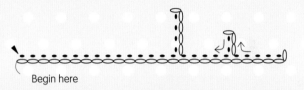

Begin here

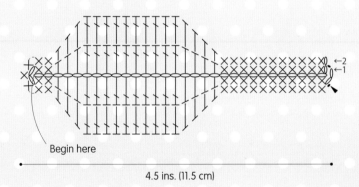

Begin here

4.5 ins. (11.5 cm)

Leaf:

Using dark green yarn, ch 31.

Row 1: Beginning with second chain from hook, sc 11, hdc 4, dc 10, hdc 3, sc 2, ch 2 and continue around other side of starting chain. Sc 2, hdc 3, dc 10, hdc 4, sc 11, ch 2, sl st.

Row 2: ch 1, sc 11, hdc 4, dc 10, hdc 3, sc 2, sc 3 around end and continue around other side, sc 2, hdc 3, dc 10, hdc 4, sc 11, sl st. Cut yarn and pull through.

Sew the Pieces Together:

Attach flowers to the stems. Place stem inside leaf and use the whipstitch to wrap the bottom of the leaf to the stem.

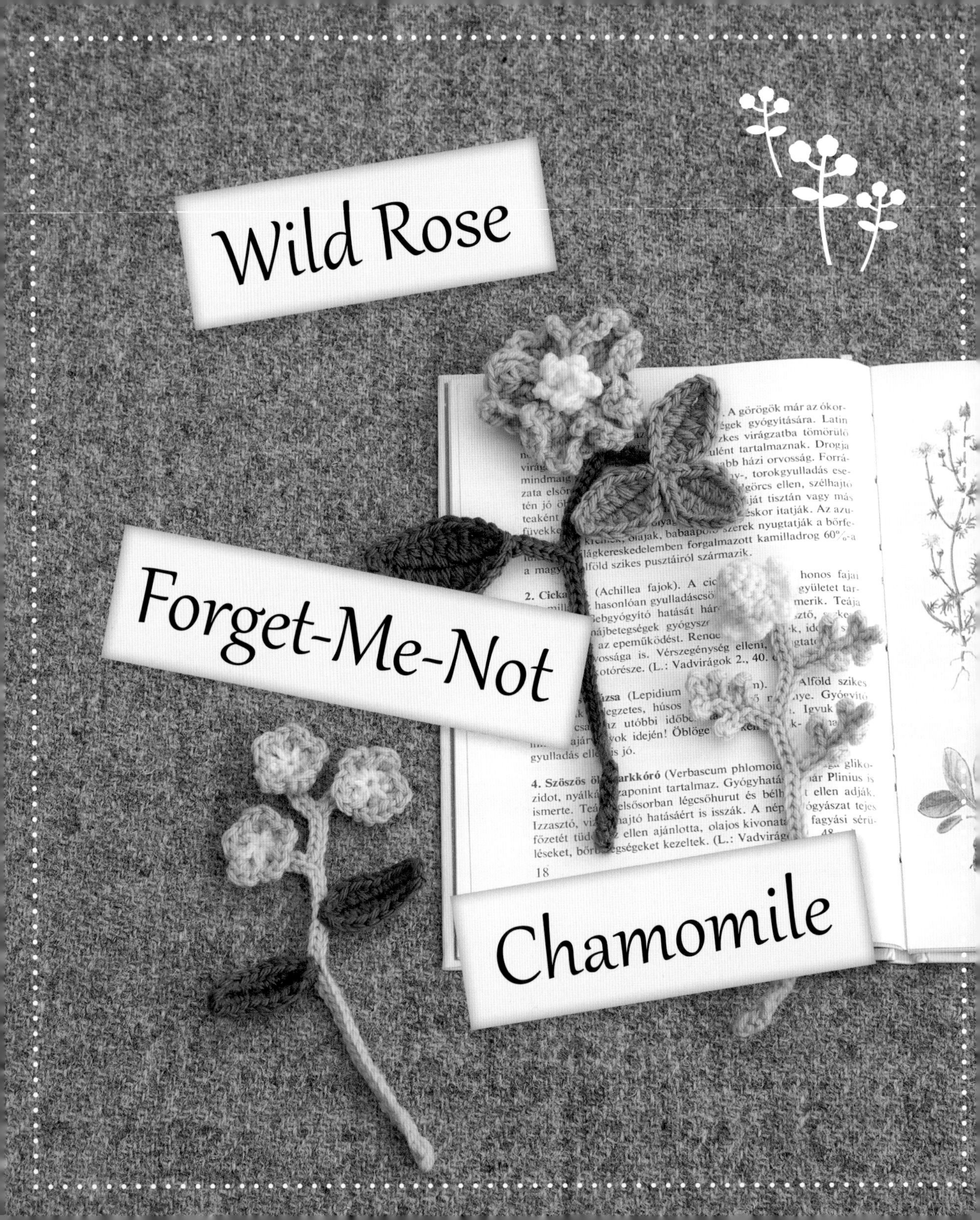
Wild Rose
Forget-Me-Not
Chamomile

Wild Rose

Materials:

- Medium-weight yarn (acrylic and wool blend) in pink, light green and dark green, 6 yds (2g)
- Medium-weight yarn (acrylic and wool blend) in white, 3 yds (1g)

Tools:

- US size C/2 (2.5 mm) crochet hook
- Tapestry or yarn needle

Stitches Used:

Crochet: chain stitch (ch), double crochet (dc), half-double crochet (hdc), single crochet (sc) and slip stitch (sl st). Piecing: whipstitch. (See pages 10–13 for detailed instructions.)

Special stitch used for this figure— triple crochet (tr): wrap yarn twice around hook, before inserting hook into stitch. Yarn over and pull through two loops. Repeat this step until only one loop remains on hook.

Forget-Me-Not

Materials:

- Medium-weight yarn (acrylic and wool blend) in light green, 6 yds (2g)
- Medium-weight yarn (acrylic and wool blend) in white and yellow, 3 yds (1g) each

Tools:

- US size C/2 (2.5 mm) crochet hook
- Tapestry or yarn needle
- Toy stuffing, small amount

Stitches Used:

Crochet: chain stitch (ch), double crochet (dc), half-double crochet (hdc), single crochet (sc), single crochet increase (sc inc) and slip stitch (sl st). Piecing: whipstitch. (See pages 10–13 for detailed stitch instructions.)

Chamomile

Materials:

- Medium-weight yarn (acrylic and wool blend) in light green, 6 yds (2g)
- Medium-weight yarn (acrylic and wool blend) in white and yellow, 3 yds (1g) each

Tools:

- US size C/2 (2.5 mm) crochet hook
- Tapestry or yarn needle
- Toy stuffing, small amount

Stitches Used:

Crochet: chain stitch (ch), double crochet (dc), half-double crochet (hdc), single crochet (sc), single crochet increase (sc inc) and slip stitch (sl st). Piecing: whipstitch. (See pages 10–13 for detailed stitch instructions.)

Wild Rose

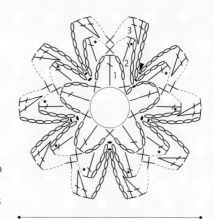

2 ins. (4.5 cm)

Flower:

Note: Refer to the chart to see where on the previous round your stitches for the next round should be placed.

Using pink yarn and the crochet-in-the-round method (see page 14 for detailed stitch instructions), make a center ring.

Round 1: ch 1, (sc 1, ch 3, dc 1, ch 3) five times. Sl st into first ch. Pull tail of center ring to close loop.

Round 2: (ch 4, dc into the ch 3 from previous row, sc 1, dc into the ch 3 from previous row, ch 4, sl st) five times.

Round 3: (ch 6, dc inc, sc 1, dc inc, ch 6, sl st) five times.

Cut yarn, leaving a 6-in. tail, and pull through.

Flower Center:

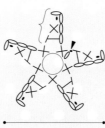

.75 in. (2 cm)

Using white yarn and the crochet-in-the-round method, make a center ring.

Round 1: sl st, (ch 5, sl st) eight times around ring. Cut yarn, leaving a 6-in. tail, and pull through. Pull tail of center ring to close loop.

Calyx :

Using dark green yarn and the crochet-in-the-round method, make a center ring.

Round 1: ch 1, sc 1, ch 4. Sl st into second chain from hook, sc 1, hdc 1. Repeat these stitches five times around the ring. Sl st into first chain, cut yarn, leaving a 6-in. tail, and pull through. Pull tail of center ring to close loop.

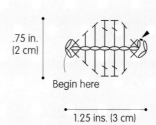

1.25 ins. (3 cm)

Leaf A (make three):

Using light green yarn, ch 8.

Row 1: Beginning with second chain from hook, sc 1, hdc 1, dc 2, hdc 2, sc 1, ch 2 and continue around other side of starting chain. Sc 1, hdc 2, dc 2, hdc 1, sc 1, ch 2, sl st. Cut yarn and pull through.

.75 in. (2 cm)

Begin here

1.25 ins. (3 cm)

Leaf B:

Using dark green yarn, ch 12.

Row 1: Beginning with second chain from hook, sc 1, hdc 2, dc 2, tr 3, dc 1, hdc 1, sc 1, ch 2 and continue around other side of starting chain. Sc 1, hdc 1, dc 1, tr 3, dc 2, hdc 2, sc 1, ch 2, sl st. Cut yarn and pull through.

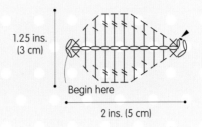

1.25 ins. (3 cm)

Begin here

2 ins. (5 cm)

Stem:

Using dark green yarn, ch 41.

Row 1: Beginning with second chain from hook, sl st 5. Ch 6, work sl st in second chain from hook, sl st 15 down new chain and continue back down starting chain. Ch 6, work sl st in second chain from hook, sl st 30 down new chain and finish down starting chain. Cut yarn and pull through.

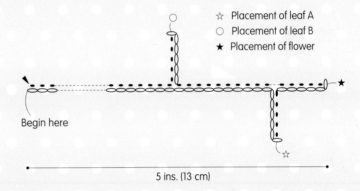

☆ Placement of leaf A
○ Placement of leaf B
★ Placement of flower

Begin here

5 ins. (13 cm)

Sew the Pieces Together:

Use the whipstitch to sew the calyx to the back of the flower, then sew the flower center to the front. Sew the three pattern A leaves together (use the diagram as reference). Attach the flower to the top of stem, three leaves to the second stem, and the pattern B leaf to the third. Weave in ends to finish.

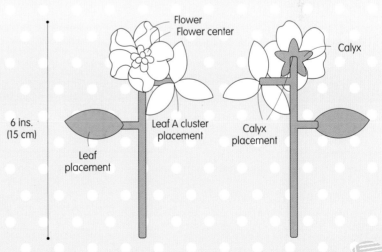

Flower
Flower center

Calyx

6 ins. (15 cm)

Leaf A cluster placement

Calyx placement

Leaf placement

Forget-Me-Not

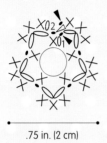

.75 in. (2 cm)

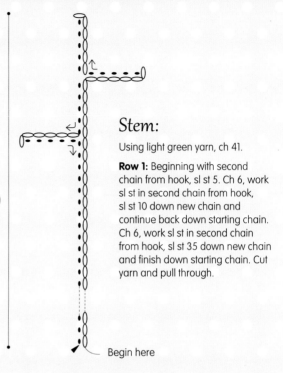

5 ins. (13 cm)

Stem:

Using light green yarn, ch 41.

Row 1: Beginning with second chain from hook, sl st 5. Ch 6, work sl st in second chain from hook, sl st 10 down new chain and continue back down starting chain. Ch 6, work sl st in second chain from hook, sl st 35 down new chain and finish down starting chain. Cut yarn and pull through.

Begin here

Flower (make three):

Using white yarn and the crochet-in-the-round method (see page 14 for detailed stitch instructions), make a center ring.

Round 1: ch 1, (sc 1, ch 2) five times. Sl st into first ch. Cut yarn and pull through. Pull tail of center ring to close loop.

Round 2: Using light blue yarn, reattach in the first sc of previous row with a sl st. Ch 1, (sc 3, sl st) five times around. Cut yarn and pull through.

Leaf (make two):

Using dark green yarn, ch 9.

Row 1: Beginning with second chain from hook, sc 4, hdc 3, sc 1, ch 2 and continue around other side of starting chain. Sc 1, hdc 3, sc 4, ch 2, sl st. Cut yarn and pull through.

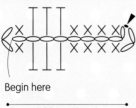

Begin here

1.25 ins. (3 cm)

Sew the Pieces Together:

Attach the flowers to top and two stems. Sew two leaves to the main stalk of the stem using the whipstitch. Weave in ends to finish.

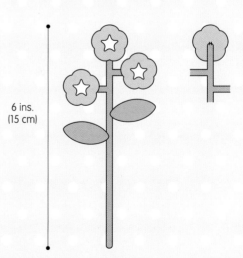

6 ins. (15 cm)

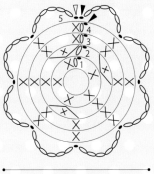

1.25 ins. (3 cm)

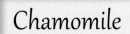

Chamomile

Flower:

Using yellow yarn and the crochet-in-the-round method (see page 14 for detailed stitch instructions), make a center ring.

Round 1: ch 1, sc 5. Pull tail of center ring to close loop, sl st in first ch.

Round 2: ch 1, (sc inc, sc 1) twice, sc inc, sl st.

Rounds 3–4: ch 1, sc 8, sl st. Cut yarn and pull through.

Round 5: Using white yarn, reattach in the first sc of previous row with a sl st. (Ch 6, sl st) times around. Cut yarn and pull through.

Stem:

Using light green yarn, ch 32.

Make a leaf: Beginning with second chain from hook, sl st 3. Ch 5, work sl st in second chain from hook, sl st 1 more down new chain. Ch 3, sl st in second chain from hook, sl st 1 more down new chain. Ch 3, sl st in second chain from hook, sl st 4 more times. Ch 4, sl st in second chain from hook, sl st 5 more down to end of chain.

Ch 17. Repeat the above steps for second leaf.

Ch 6, beginning with second chain from hook, sl st 10.

Ch 7. Repeat the above steps for third leaf. Sl st 30 back down main stem. Cut yarn and pull through.

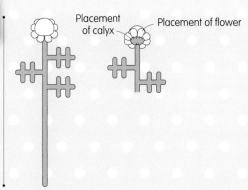

5 ins. (13 cm)

Begin here

Calyx:

Using light green yarn and the crochet-in-the-round method, make a center ring.

Round 1: ch 1, sc 5. Pull tail of center ring to close loop, sl st in first ch.

Round 2: ch 1, (sc inc, sc 1) twice, sc inc, sl st. Cut yarn and pull through.

Did you know? "Calyx" is the word for the part that connects the flower to the stem.

Placement of calyx

Placement of flower

6 ins. (15 cm)

Sew the Pieces Together:

Stuff the calyx with a small amount of toy stuffing and use the whipstitch to attach to the back of the flower. Attach the flower to top of stem. Weave in ends to finish.

Dried Flowers

Clover

Materials:

- Medium-weight yarn (acrylic and wool blend) in light green, dark green and white, 6 yds (2g) each

Tools:

- US size C/2 (2.5 mm) crochet hook
- Tapestry or yarn needle

Stitches Used:

Crochet: chain stitch (ch), double crochet (dc), half-double crochet (hdc), single crochet (sc) and slip stitch (sl st). (See pages 10–13 for detailed stitch instructions.)

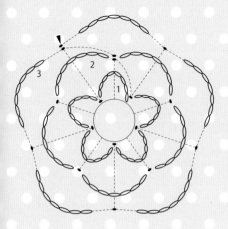

Clover:

Using white yarn and the crochet-in-the-round method (see page 14 for detailed stitch instructions), make a center ring.

Round 1: (ch 8, sl st into center ring) five times. Pull tail of center ring to partially close loop, sl st in first ch. *Note: Don't close the loop fully as you will need to sl st into it in round 2.*

Round 2: sl st in to center ring between the first two sl sts of round 1. *Note: Make sure you work underneath the chains from round 1.* Ch 7, sl st between the second and third sl sts of previous round. Repeat four more times. Sl st in first sl st of round.

Round 3: Continue to work underneath the chains, sl st into first sl st from round 1. Ch 7, sl st into second sl st from round 1. Repeat four more times, sl st in first sl st of round. Cut yarn and pull through. Pull the tail of center ring tightly to finish.

Three-Leaf Clover:

Using light green yarn and the crochet-in-the-round method, make a center ring.

Round 1: (ch 2, hdc 1, ch 2, sl st.) three times. Cut yarn and pull through. Pull tail of center ring to close loop.

Round 2: Use the chart for reference on stitch placement. Using dark green yarn, reattach in the first sl st of previous row. (Ch 4, dc 1, sc 1, dc 1, ch 4, sl st) three times. Cut yarn and pull through.

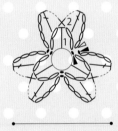

1.25 ins. (3.5 cm)

1.5 ins. (4 cm)

Four-Leaf Clover:

Begin with rounds 1 and 2 for the three leaf clover; repeat steps four times instead of three. At end of round 2, ch 12. Starting with second chain from hook, sl st 11 back down the chain. Cut yarn and pull through.

Weave in ends to finish.

Ladybugs

Materials:

- Medium-weight yarn (acrylic and wool blend) in red or orange, 6 yds (2g)
- Medium-weight yarn (acrylic and wool blend) in black and white, 6 yds each (2g)

Stitches Used:

Crochet: chain stitch (ch), double crochet (dc), half-double crochet (hdc), single crochet (sc), slip stitch (sl st) and through the back loop (tbl). Piecing: whipstitch. (See pages 10–13 for detailed stitch instructions.)

Tools:

- US size C/2 (2.5 mm) crochet hook
- Tapestry or yarn needle
- Toy stuffing, small amount
- Locking stitch marker

Body:

Using red or orange yarn and the crochet-in-the-round method (see page 14 for detailed stitch instructions), make a center ring.

Round 1: ch 1, sc 5, sl st into first ch. Pull tail of center ring to close loop. Mark first stitch with a locking stitch marker to indicate the beginning of your rounds.

Round 2: ch 1, (sc inc) five times, sl st.

Round 3: ch 1, (sc 1, sc inc) five times, sl st.

Rounds 4–5: ch 1, sc 15, sl st.

Round 6: *Note: Work all sts of this round tbl.* Ch 1, (sc 1, sc2tog) five times, sl st.

Round 7: ch 1, (sc2tog) five times, sl st. Cut yarn, leaving a 6-in. tail, and pull through.

Head:

Using black yarn and the crochet-in-the-round method, make a center ring.

Round 1: ch 1, sc 6. Pull tail of center ring to close loop, sl st. Cut yarn, leaving a 6-in. tail, and pull through.

Details:

Referring to the diagram for placement, embroider spots with white yarn. Pass yarn needle from back to front. Catch one stitch and pass the needle from back to front. Then pass the needle back to where you started to create the V shape. Stuff body with small amount of toy stuffing and close up opening. Use the whipstitch to attach head to body. Weave in any ends to finish your ladybug.

How to embroider spots

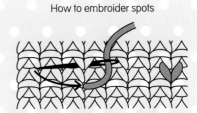

1 in. (2.5 cm)

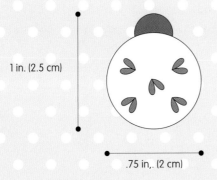

.75 in,. (2 cm)

The Sweetest Things

Cup & Saucer

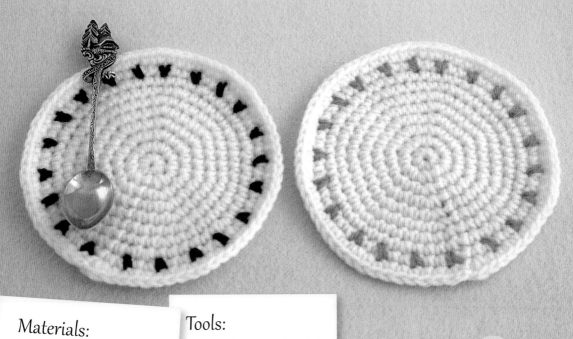

Materials:

- Medium-weight yarn (acrylic and wool blend) in white, 55 yds (22g)
- Medium-weight yarn (acrylic and wool blend) in red or blue, 3 yds (1g)

Tools:

- US size E/4 (3.5 mm) crochet hook
- Tapestry or yarn needle
- Locking stitch marker

Stitches Used:

Crochet: chain stitch (ch), single crochet (sc), single crochet increase (sc inc) and slip stitch (sl st). Details: embroidery. (See pages 10–13 for detailed stitch instructions.)

Cup:

Using white yarn and the crochet-in-the-round method (see page 14 for detailed stitch instructions), make a center ring.

Round 1: ch 1, sc 7. Pull tail of center ring to close loop, sl st in first ch. Place a locking stitch marker at the first stitch of the round; move it up each round to help you keep track of your rounds.

Round 2: ch 1, (sc inc) seven times, sl st.

Round 3: ch 1, (sc 1, sc inc) seven times, sl st.

Round 4: ch 1, (sc 2, sc inc) seven times, sl st.

Round 5: ch 1, sc 28, sl st.

Round 6: ch 1, (sc 3, sc inc) seven times, sl st.

Round 7: ch 1, sc 35, sl st.

Round 8: ch 1, (sc 4, sc inc) seven times, sl st.

Rounds 9–11: ch 1, sc 42, sl st.

Round 12: ch 1, (sc 13, sc inc) three times, sl st.

Rounds 13–14: ch 1, sc 45, sl st. Cut yarn and pull through.

Saucer:

Using white yarn and the crochet-in-the-round method, make a center ring.

Round 1: ch 1, sc 7. Pull tail of center ring to close loop, sl st in first ch.

Round 2: ch 1, (sc inc) seven times, sl st.

Round 3: ch 1, (sc 1, sc inc) seven times, sl st.

Round 4: ch 1, (sc 2, sc inc) seven times, sl st.

Round 5: ch 1, (sc 3, sc inc) seven times, sl st.

Round 6: ch 1, (sc 4, sc inc) seven times, sl st.

Round 7: ch 1, sc 3, sc inc (sc 5, sc inc) six times, sc 2, sl st.

Round 8: ch 1, sc 2, sc inc (sc 6, sc inc) six times, sc 4, sl st.

Round 9: ch 1, sc 1, sc inc (sc 7, sc inc) six times, sc 6, sl st.

Round 10: ch 1, sc inc (sc 8, sc inc) six times, sc 8, sl st. Cut yarn and pull through.

Handle:

Using white yarn, ch 16.

Row 1: sc 15. Cut yarn leaving a long tail and pull through.

Piecing and Details:

Use the red or blue yarn to embroider designs in the second row from top. Pass yarn needle from back to front. Catch one stitch and pass the needle from back to front. Then pass the needle back to where you started to create the V shape. Repeat this around both the cup and saucer on every third stitch.

Sew the handle to the top and bottom cup at the seam. Weave in all ends to finish your tea-service setting.

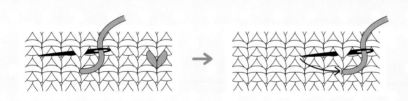

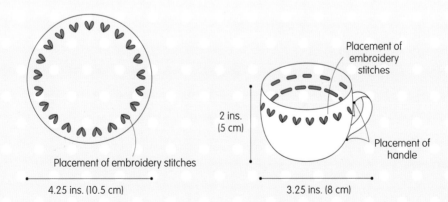

Placement of embroidery stitches

Placement of embroidery stitches

4.25 ins. (10.5 cm)

2 ins. (5 cm)

Placement of handle

3.25 ins. (8 cm)

Spoon & Fork

Materials:

- Medium-weight yarn (acrylic and wool blend) in white, 6 yds (2g) for each utensil.

Tools:

- US size C/2 (2.5 mm) crochet hook
- Tapestry or yarn needle

Stitches Used:

Crochet: chain stitch (ch), double crochet (dc), half-double crochet (hdc), single crochet (sc) and slip stitch (sl st). (See page 10–13 for detailed stitch instructions.)

Special stitches used for this figure—double crochet three together (dc3tog): (Yarn over, insert hook in next stitch, yarn over and pull loop through, yarn over, draw through two loops on hook) three times (four loops remaining on hook), yarn over, draw through all loops on hook—two stitches decreased.

Single crochet triple increase (sc3inc): single crochet three times into the same stitch.

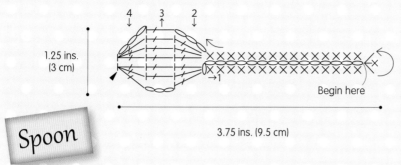

**1.25 ins.
(3 cm)**

Begin here

Spoon

3.75 ins. (9.5 cm)

Begin with ch 16.

Row 1: Beginning with second chain from hook, sc 15, sc3inc then continue around other side of starting chain. Sc 15.

Row 2: ch 3, dc 6.

Row 3: ch 3, dc 6.

Row 4: ch 3, (dc3tog) twice. Cut yarn and pull through. Weave in ends to finish.

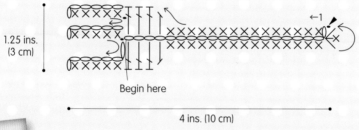

**1.25 ins.
(3 cm)**

Begin here

4 ins. (10 cm)

Fork

Begin with ch 20.

Row 1: Beginning with second chain from hook, sc 15, hdc 1, dc 3.

Tines: (ch 6, beginning with second chain from hook sc 5, sl st) twice, ch 1, then repeat one more time.

Then continue around other side of starting chain, dc 3, hdc 1, sc 15, sc triple inc, sl st. Cut yarn and pull through. Weave in ends to finish.

Macarons

Materials:

- Medium-weight yarn (acrylic and wool blend) in your choice of cookie color, 10 yds (3g)
- Medium-weight yarn (acrylic and wool blend) in your choice of filling color, 3 yds (1g)

Tools:

- US size C/2 (2.5 mm) crochet hook
- Tapestry or yarn needle
- Toy stuffing, small amount

Stitches Used:

Crochet: chain stitch (ch), single crochet (sc), single crochet increase (sc inc), slip stitch (sl st) and through the back loop (tbl). Piecing: whipstitch. (See pages 10–13 for detailed stitch instructions.)

Macaron Top/Bottom (make two):

Using your choice of cookie color and the crochet-in-the-round method (see page 14 for detailed stitch instructions), make a center ring.

Round 1: ch 1, sc 7. Pull tail of center ring to close loop, sl st in first ch.

Round 2: ch 1, (sc inc) seven times, sl st.

Round 3: ch 1, (sc 1, sc inc) seven times, sl st.

Round 4: ch 1, (sc inc, sc 2) seven times, sl st.

Rounds 5–6: ch 1, sc 28, sl st. *Note: Round 6 only, work tbl.*

Round 7: ch 1, (sc2tog, sc 2) seven times, sl st.

Round 8: ch 1, (sc2tog, sc 1) seven times, sl st. Cut yarn and pull through.

Macaron Filling:

Using your choice of cookie color and the crochet-in-the-round method, make a center ring.

Round 1: ch 1, sc 7. Pull tail of center ring to close loop, sl st in first ch.

Round 2: ch 1, (sc inc) seven times, sl st.

Round 3: ch 1, (sc 1, sc inc) seven times, sl st.

Round 4: ch 1, (sc inc, sc 2) seven times, sl st.

Rounds 5–6: ch 1, sc 28, sl st. *Note: Round 6 only, work tbl.*

Round 7: ch 1, (sc2tog, sc 2) seven times, sl st.

Round 8: ch 1, (sc2tog, sc 1) seven times, sl st. Cut yarn and pull through.

Finishing:

Stuff each macaron half with a small amount of toy stuffing. Sandwich the filling piece in between the two macaron halves and sew all three together (refer to the diagram for the best way to do this). Weave in ends to finish.

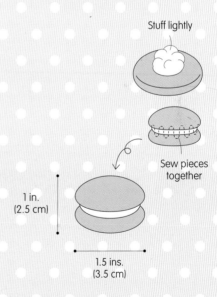

Stuff lightly

Sew pieces together

1 in. (2.5 cm)

1.5 ins. (3.5 cm)

Cupcakes

Materials:

- Medium-weight yarn (acrylic and wool blend) in brown, tan or pink for cake, 20 yds (8g)
- Medium-weight yarn (acrylic and wool blend) in white, chocolate brown or pastel yellow for icing, 8 yds (3g) each
- Medium-weight yarn (acrylic and wool blend) in reds for berries, 3 yds (1g) each
- Medium-weight yarn (acrylic and wool blend) in green, small amount for stems or leaves
- Bulky-weight yarn (acrylic and nylon blend) in white, small amount for whipped cream

Tools:

- US size C/2 (2.5 mm), D/3 (3 mm), E/4 (3.5 mm), H/8 (5 mm) crochet hook
- Tapestry or yarn needle
- Toy stuffing, small amount
- Locking stitch marker

Stitches Used:

Crochet: chain stitch (ch), double crochet (dc), double crochet increase (dc inc), half-double crochet (hdc), single crochet (sc), single crochet increase (sc inc) slip stitch (sl st) and through the back loop (tbl). (See pages 10–13 for detailed stitch instructions.)

Cake:

Use the E/4 crochet hook and your choice of cake color yarn. Begin with the crochet-in-the-round method (see page 14 for detailed stitch instructions) and make a center ring.

Round 1: ch 1, sc 7, sl st.

Round 2: ch 1, (sc inc) seven times, sl st.

Round 3: ch 1, (sc 1, sc inc) six times, sc 2, sl st.

Round 4: *Note: Work all sts of this round tbl.* Ch 1, sc 20, sl st.

Round 5: ch 1, sc 20, sl st.

Round 6: ch 1, (sc 4, sc inc) four times, sl st.

Round 7: ch 1, sc 24, sl st.

Round 8: ch 1, sc 2, sc inc, (sc 5, sc inc) three times, sc 3, sl st.

Round 9: ch 1, sc 28, sl st.

Round 10: ch 1, (sc 6, sc inc) four times, sl st.

Round 11: ch 1, sc 32, sl st.

Round 12: *Note: Work all sts of this round tbl.* Ch 1, (sc 2, sc2tog) eight times, sl st.

Round 13: ch 1, sc 24, sl st.

Round 14: ch 1, (sc 1, sc2tog) eight times, sl st.

Round 15: ch 1, (sc2tog) eight times, sl st. Cut yarn leaving a long tail and pull through.

Icing:

Use the D/3 crochet hook and your choice of icing color yarn. Begin with the crochet-in-the-round method and make a center ring.

Round 1: ch 1, sc 9, sl st. Mark first stitch with a locking stitch marker to indicate the beginning of your rounds.

Round 2: ch 3, dc into same stitch as turning chain, (dc inc) eight times, sl st.

Round 3: ch 3, (dc inc, dc 1) eight times, dc inc, sl st.

Round 4: ch 1, (sc 1, ch 3, dc 2) in first stitch. (Skip two stitches, sc 1, ch 3, dc 2) eight times, sl st. Cut yarn, leaving a long tail, and pull through.

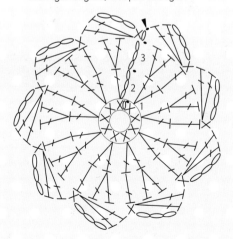

Toppings:

Use the C/2 crochet hook for all berries.

Cherry:

Using your choice of berry color yarn and the crochet-in-the-round method, make a center ring.

Round 1: ch 1, sc 6, sl st.

Round 2: ch 1, (sc inc) six times, sl st.

Rounds 3 - 6: ch 1, sc 12, sl st.

Round 7: ch 1, (sc2tog) six times, sl st. Cut yarn and pull through.

Stem:

Using green yarn, ch 9.

Row 1: Beginning in second chain from hook, sl st 8. Cut yarn and pull through.

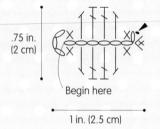

.75 in. (2 cm)

1 in. (2.5 cm)

Begin here

Red Berry (make three):

Using your choice of yarn color for the berries, begin with crochet-in-the-round method, make a center ring.

Round 1: ch 1, sc 6, sl st.

Round 2: ch 1, (sc 1, sc inc) three times, sl st.

Rounds 3 & 4: ch 1, sc 9, sl st.

Round 5: ch 1, (sc2tog) four times, sc 1, sl st. Cut yarn and pull through.

Leaf (make three):

Using green yarn, ch 7.

Row 1: Beginning in second chain from hook, sc 1, hdc 1, dc 2, hdc 1, sc 1. Ch 3 then continue down other side of starting chain, sc 1, hdc 1, dc 2, hdc 1, sc 1, sc inc, sl st. Cut yarn and pull through.

Whipped Cream:

Using the bulky white yarn with the H/8 crochet hook, ch 10. Sl st into first ch to create a ring. Cut yarn and pull through.

Miniature Strawberry:

Using your choice of red yarn shade and the crochet-in-the-round method, make a center ring.

Round 1: ch 1, sc 6, sl st.

Round 2: ch 1, (sc 1, sc inc) three times, sl st.

Round 3: ch 1, sc 9, sl st.

Round 4: ch 1, (sc 2, sc inc) three times, sl st.

Rounds 5–7: ch 1, sc 12, sl st.

Round 8: ch 1, (sc2tog) six times, sl st. Cut yarn and pull through.

Leafy Top:

Using green yarn, begin with crochet-in-the-round method and make a center ring.

Round 1: ch 1, sc 5, sl st.

Round 2: (ch 3, dc 1, ch 3, sl st) five times. Cut yarn and pull through.

Sew the Pieces Together:

Fill the cake piece with toy stuffing. Don't overffill or your cupcake won't sit flat. Place icing on top, and sew to row 12 of cake. Stuff the berries with toy stuffing and attach leaves. For the cherry, insert end of stem into top and sew closed. Sew berries to top of cupcake. For strawberry, attach the whipped cream first, then affix the strawberry to the top of the cream. Weave in any ends to finish.

Where to sew icing to cupcake

Placing and sewing berries to icing

Doughnuts

Materials (per doughnut):

- Medium-weight yarn (acrylic and wool blend) in light yellow, 20 yds (8g) for doughnut
- Medium-weight yarn (acrylic and wool blend) in brown, light brown or white, 20 yds (8g) for frosting

Tools:

- US size E/4 (3.5 mm) crochet hook
- Tapestry or yarn needle
- Toy stuffing, 10g

Stitches Used:

Crochet: chain stitch (ch), single crochet (sc), single crochet increase (sc inc), single crochet decrease (sc2tog) and slip stitch (sl st). Piecing: whipstitch. (See pages 10–13 for detailed stitch instructions.)

Doughnut:

Using your frosting color, begin with ch 18. Sl st into first ch to make a center ring, continue with the crochet-in-the-round method.

Round 1: This row only, sc into the top half and back loop of the starting chain (see diagram). Ch 1, sc 18, sl st.

Round 2: ch 1, sc 18, sl st.

Round 3: ch 1, (sc 2, sc inc) six times, sl st.

Round 4: ch 1, (sc 3, sc inc) six times, sl st.

Round 5: ch 1, sc 1, sc inc, (sc 4, sc inc) five times, sc 3, sl st.

Round 6: ch 1, (sc 5, sc inc) six times, sl st.

Round 7: ch 1, sc 42, sl st.

Round 8: This row only, carry the yarn color not in use horizontally across the stitches and crochet over the strand with the working yarn to hide it. Ch 1 (sc 3 in frosting color, sc 3 in yellow) seven times. Continue with yellow yarn, sl st.

Rounds 9–10: ch 1, sc 42, sl st.

Round 11: ch 1, (sc 5, sc2tog) six times, sl st.

Round 12: ch 1, sc 2, sc2tog, (sc 4, sc2tog) five times, sc 2, sl st.

Round 13: ch 1, (sc 3, sc2tog) six times, sl st.

Round 14: ch 1, (sc 2, sc2tog) six times, sl st.

Round 15: ch 1, sc 18, sl st. Cut yarn, leaving a long tail, and pull through.

Diagram for row 1

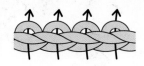

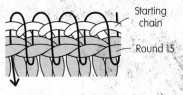

Starting chain

Round 15

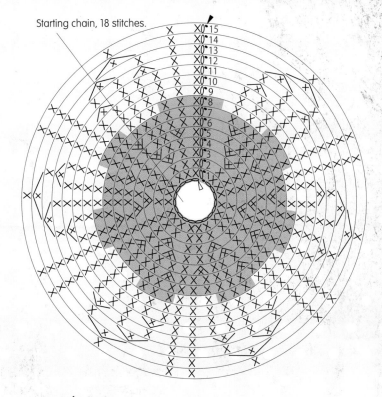

Starting chain, 18 stitches.

Finishing:

Stuff doughnut with toy stuffing. Use the tail of your piece to whipstitch row 15 to the beginning chain (see above diagram). Weave in all ends.

Candy

Need a basket for your candy?

Make the pattern on page 120 in a soft brown.

Materials:

- Medium-weight yarn (acrylic and wool blend) in color of your choice, 6 yds (2g)

Tools:

- US size C/2 (2.5 mm) crochet hook
- Tapestry or yarn need
- Toy stuffing, small amount
- Locking stitch marker

Stitches Used:

Crochet: chain stitch (ch), double crochet (dc), single crochet (sc), single crochet increase (sc inc), single crochet decrease (sc2tog) and slip stitch (sl st). (See pages 10–13 for detailed stitch instructions.)

Special stitches/techniques used for this figure—V-Stitch (v-st): (dc, ch 1, dc) all in the same stitch.

Crochet around the chain: Instead of crocheting into both loops of the chain, reach below the starting chain, go in the space between the stitches and grab the yarn to work the stitch.

Candy, Side A:

Begin with ch 6. Sl st into first ch to make a center ring, continue with the crochet-in-the-round method (see detailed instructions on page 14).

Round 1: Crochet around the chain, ch 1, sc 6, sl st.

Round 2: ch 1, (sc inc) six times, sl st.

Rounds 3–6: ch 1, sc 12, sl st.

Round 7: ch 1, (sc2tog) six times, sl st. Sutff candy with small amount of toy stuffing here.

Round 8: ch 4, dc 1 into first stitch, (v-st) five times, sl st. Cut yarn and pull through.

Center chain

Candy, Side B:

Reattach yarn at beginning end of Side A. Ch 4, dc 1 into first stitch, (v-st) five times, sl st. Cut yarn and pull through.

Finishing:

Tie a piece of yarn around the two smallest parts of candy and pull tight. Weave in all ends

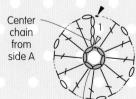

Center chain from side A

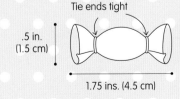

Tie ends tight

.5 in. (1.5 cm)

1.75 ins. (4.5 cm)

Winter Holidays

Příjemné svátky vánoční

Bells!
Bells!
Bells!

Stockings
& Booties

Bells! Bells! Bells!

Materials:

- Medium-weight yarn (acrylic and wool blend) in red, yellow or white, 15 yds (5g) for each bell body
- Medium-weight yarn (acrylic and wool blend) in white or yellow, 3 yds (1g) for each bell clapper

Tools:

- US size C/2 (2.5 mm) and D/3 (3 mm) crochet hooks
- Tapestry or yarn needle
- Ribbon (optional for embellishment)

Stitches Used:

Crochet: chain stitch (ch), double crochet cluster (dc CL), single crochet (sc), single crochet increase (sc inc), single crochet decrease (sc2tog) and slip stitch (sl st). (See pages 10–13 for detailed crochet stitch instructions.)

Bell body:

Use red or yellow yarn and D/3 hook. Begin with the crochet-in-the-round method (see page 14 for detailed stitch instructions) and make a center ring. Leave a long tail to make loop later.

Round 1: ch 1, sc5, sl st into top of the starting chain. Pull tail of center ring to close loop.

Round 2: ch 1, (sc inc) five times, sl st.

Round 3: ch 1, (sc 1, sc inc) five times, sl st.

Round 4: ch 1, (sc 2, sc inc) five times, sl st.

Rounds 5-10: ch 1, sc 20, sl st.

Round 11: ch 1, (sc 1, sc inc) ten times, sl st.

Round 12: ch 1, sc 30, sl st. Cut yarn, leaving a 6-in. tail, and pull though.

Bell Clapper:

Using contrasting color and C/2 hook, begin with ch 14.

Clapper end: dc CL into fourth ch from hook, ch 3, dc CL into same ch as the first.

Cut yarn, leaving a 6-in. tail, and pull through.

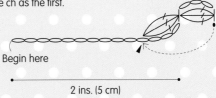

Begin here

2 ins. (5 cm)

Bell:

Use red or white yarn and D/3 hook. Begin with the crochet-in-the-round method and make a center ring. Leave a long tail to make loop later.

Round 1: ch 1, sc5, sl st into top of the starting chain. Pull tail of center ring to close loop.

Round 2: ch 1, (sc inc) five times, sl st.

Round 3: ch 1, (sc 1, sc inc) five times, sl st.

Rounds 4–7: ch 1, sc 15, sl st.

Round 8: ch 1, (sc 1, sc inc) seven times, sc inc, sl st.

Round 9: ch 1, sc 23, sl st. Cut yarn, leaving a 6-in. tail, and pull through.

chain 10 for loop

2 ins. (5 cm)

1.5 ins. (3.5 cm)

Finishing details:

To make top loop, use the long tail you left at the beginning, ch 15 for large bell and 10 for the small bell. Make loop with a sl st into the first chain.

Sew the clapper to the inside top of the large bell. Weave in any ends to finish both bells. Add ribbon bow if desired.

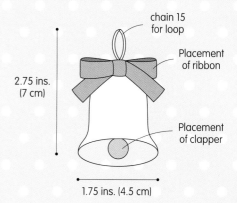

chain 15 for loop

Placement of ribbon

2.75 ins. (7 cm)

Placement of clapper

1.75 ins. (4.5 cm)

Stockings & Booties

Materials:

- Medium-weight yarn (acrylic and wool blend) in red, 12 yds (4g) for each stocking/bootie
- Medium-weight yarn (acrylic and wool blend) in white, 3 yds (1g) for each stocking/bootie
- Pompoms, 4 .25-in. balls (for boots only)

Tools:

- US size E/4 (3.5 mm) crochet hook
- Tapestry or yarn needle

Stitches Used:

Crochet: chain stitch (ch), single crochet (sc), single crochet increase (sc inc), single crochet decrease (sc2tog) and slip stitch (sl st). (See pages 10–13 for detailed crochet stitch instructions.)

Special stitches used for this figure—Single crochet triple decrease (sc3tog): Draw a loop through first stitch (do NOT yarn over and complete stitch), then insert the hook into the second stitch and pull through, repeat one more time on a third stitch. You will have four loops on the hook. Yarn over and pull through all four loops.

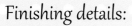

Basic Stocking:

Using red yarn and the crochet-in-the-round method, make a center ring.

Toe:

Round 1: ch 1, sc 7, sl st into top of the starting chain. Pull tail of center ring to close loop.

Round 2: ch 1, (sc inc) seven times, sl st.

Rounds 3–7: ch 1, sc 14, sl st.

Heel:

Rows 8–11: Note: these rows and row 12 are worked back and forth—they ARE NOT in the round. Ch 1, sc 7.

Row 12: ch 1, (sc 1, sc2tog) twice, sc 1. Cut yarn leaving an 8-in. tail, and pull though. Fold the back of the heel piece in half and use the whipstitch to close.

Leg:

Reattach yarn in the back of the heel. Pick up 4 stitches on either side of heel for round 13.

Round 13: ch 1, sc 4, (sc3tog, sc 1) three times, sc 3, sl st.

Rounds 14–18: ch 1, sc 14, sl st.

Round 19: ch 1, sc inc, sc 6, sc inc, sc 5, sl st.

Rounds 20–21: ch 1, sc 15, sl st. At the end of round 21, cut yarn, leaving an 8-in. tail, and pull though.

Use the same basic pattern for all of the stockings and booties, with the following variations—

For stocking A: Use white yarn for rounds 14–15, and 18–19.

For stocking B: Use white yarn for rounds 19–21.

For stocking C: Use white yarn for rows 8–12.

For booties: Use white yarn for rows 19–21, then fold them over and sew two pompoms to the front of each.

To finish, weave in any ends. Leave a loop on the top if desired.

Stocking A   Stocking B   Stocking C   Booty

All stockings are 2 ins. x 2 ins. (5 cm x 5 cm)

Booty is 2 ins. x 1.75 ins. (5 x 4 cm)

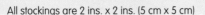

Baby's Holiday Shoes

FOCUS ON TECHNIQUE:
Crochet Around a Starting Chain

Many patterns are created in the round, not by using a center ring, but by crocheting around both sides of a starting chain. Here we show you, step by step, how to work this technique to create this adorable pair of holiday baby shoes. With intricate patterns like this, it is a good idea to keep referring to the crochet photos to see where the stitches in the new round will fall on the previous round.

Materials:
- Medium-weight yarn (acrylic and wool blend) in red, 47 yds (20g),

Measurements:
Finished piece, 3.75 x 2 x 1.5 ins. (9.5 x 5 x 4 cm)

Note that measurements are approximate and will vary due to tension and yarn choice.

Tools:
- US size D/3 (3 mm) crochet hook
- Tapestry or yarn needle
- Two buttons (.5 in)

Pattern Notes:
This pattern is worked in the round using a starting chain as a base. It is created in two pieces that are attached afterwards. The simplified pattern with out the step-by-step instructions is also included here.

Stitches Used:
Crochet: chain stitch (ch), double crochet (dc), double crochet increase (dc inc), double crochet decrease (dc2tog), half-double crochet (hdc), single crochet (sc), single crochet increase (sc inc), and slip stitch (sl st). (See pages 10–13 for detailed stitch instructions.)

Make the Starting Chain:

1 Begin with ch 13.

2 Ch 3 more for the starting ch.

3 **Begin round 1 with a double crochet:** yarn over, insert hook from front to top fifth chain from hook, yarn over.

4 Pull through. Yarn over again and pull through two loops as shown in photo.

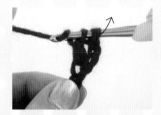

5 Yarn over and pull through remaining loops.

6 First double crochet stitch is complete.

7 Continue round 1: Work double crochet while catching cast-on chain stitches. Dc 11, at last starting chain stitch, dc 7 in same stitch. This will bring you around to the other side of the starting chain.

8 Dc 11, then dc 6 in last ch of the starting chain. This will bring you back around to the beginning.

9 Sl st in to third ch of turning chain to complete round 1.

10 **Round 2:** ch 1, sc inc. (Star marks the beginning of round)

11 Continue round 2: sc 3, hdc 4, dc 4.

12 (dc inc) seven times around the toe.

13 Finish round 2: dc 4, hdc 4, sc 3, (sc inc) six times, sl st.

14 **Round 3:** ch 3, dc 49, sl st.

15 **Round 4:** ch 3, dc 14.

16 Dc2tog as follows: Insert hook in next stitch as if making a double crochet and pull yarn through. Yarn over and pull through 2 loops on hook. Insert hook into next stitch and pull yarn through.

17 Yarn over and pull through 2 loops on hook. Yarn over and pull through all loops on hook to finish decrease.

18 Continue round 4: dc 1, (dc2tog) twice, dc 1, dc2tog, dc 17, (dc2tog, dc 2) twice, sl st to complete round 4.

19 **Round 5:** ch 3, dc 10, (dc2tog twice, dc 1) three times, dc 18, sl st. Round 6: ch 1, sc 9, hdc 3, (dc2tog) three times, hdc 3, sc 17, sl st.

Round 7: ch 1, sc 35, sl st.

20 Cut yarn, leaving a 6-in. tail, and pull through. Using yarn needle, weave in ends.

Make the Strap and Sew the Pieces Together

1 To begin, ch 17.

Row 1: Starting in second chain from hook, and crocheting into the back loop only, sc 16.

Row 2: sc 2, ch 3, sc 11. (This creates the buttonhole. Be sure to skip the three stitches of the previous row under the ch 3.)

2 Cut yarn and pull through, leaving a 12-in. tail.

3 Use the long tail left to sew strap to shoe leaving an opening with nine stitches around the front. Sew button on to side of shoe to finish.

Simplified Pattern and Charts:

Using red yarn, begin with ch 16 (includes 3 for tch).

Round 1: Beginning in fifth chain from hook, dc 11, dc 7 in end chain and continue around other side of starting chain, dc 11, dc 6 in next chain , sl st in top ch of tch.

Round 2: ch 1, sc inc, sc 3, hdc 4, dc 4, (dc inc) seven times, dc 4, hdc 4, sc 3, (sc inc) six times, sl st.

Round 3: ch 3, dc 49, sl st.

Round 4: ch 3, dc 14, dc2tog, sc 1, (dc2tog) twice, dc 1, dc2tog, dc 17, (dc2tog, dc 2) twice, sl st.

Round 5: ch 3, dc 10, (dc2tog twice, dc 1) three times, dc 18, sl st.

Round 6: ch 1, sc 9, hdc 3, (dc2tog) three times, hdc 3, sc 17, sl st.

Round 7: ch 1, sc 35, sl st. Cut yarn and pull through.

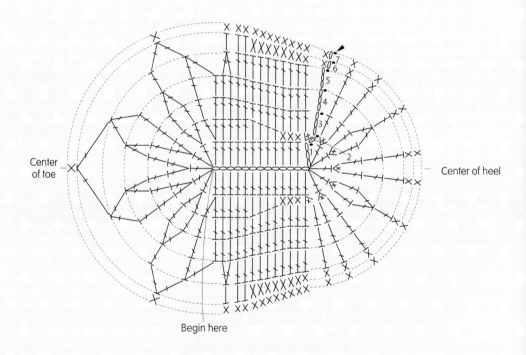

Center of toe

Center of heel

Begin here

Simply Adorable Crochet

Strap (make two):

Begin with ch 17. Crochet into the back loop of the starting chain.

Row 1: beginning in second chain from hook, sc 16, ch 1.

Row 2: sc 2, ch 3, sc 11. Cut yarn, leaving a 12-in. tail, and pull through.

This pattern can work for actual baby booties! Use a baby friendly cotton or acrylic yarn in pink or blue to make a nice gift for a new little person.

Sew the Pieces Together:

Sew strap to shoe towards the front, leaving a space of about nine stitches. Sew button to shoe underneath where the buttonhole sits. Weave in any ends to finish.

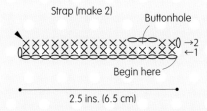

Strap (make 2)

Buttonhole

Begin here

2.5 ins. (6.5 cm)

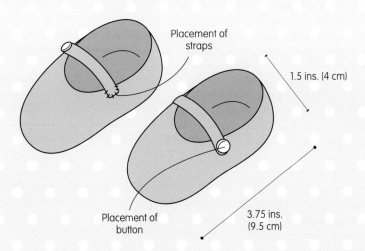

Placement of straps

Placement of button

1.5 ins. (4 cm)

3.75 ins. (9.5 cm)

Let It Snow!

Holly Jolly Wreath

Let It Snow

Materials:

- Medium-weight yarn (acrylic and wool blend) in white, 10 yds (3g) for each snowflake.

Tools:

- US size C/2 (2.5 mm) crochet hook
- Tapestry or yarn needle

Stitches Used:

Crochet: chain stitch (ch), double crochet (dc), double crochet cluster (dc CL), single crochet (sc), popcorn stitch (pc) and slip stitch (sl st). (See pages 10–13 for detailed crochet stitch instructions.)

Special stitches used for this figure—Triple crochet (tr): wrap yarn twice around hook, before inserting hook into stitch. Yarn over and pull through two loops. Repeat this step until only one loop remains on hook.

Picot stitch (p): chain 3, insert your hook into the first ch made, then sl st.

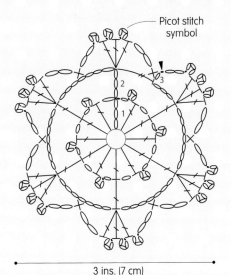

Picot stitch symbol

Snowflake A:

Note: Refer to the chart to see where on the previous round your stitches for the next round should be placed.

Using the crochet-in-the-round method (see page 14 for detailed stitch instructions), make a center ring.

Round 1: ch 3, (ch 1, dc 1, p, ch 1, dc 1) six times. Sl st into top of the starting chain. Pull tail of center ring to close loop.

Round 2: ch 3, (ch 7, dc into the second dc from previous row) five times, ch 3, tr 1 into top of starting chain.

Round 3: ch 1, sc 1, (ch 2, {dc 1, p} three times, ch 2, sc 1 into fourth chain from previous row) six times, sl st.

Cut yarn, leaving a 6-in. tail, and pull through. Weave in ends to finish.

3 ins. (7 cm)

Snowflake B (top left in photo):

Note: Refer to the chart to see where on the previous round your stitches for the next round should be placed.

Using the crochet-in-the-round method, make a center ring.

Round 1: ch 1, (sc 1, ch 3) six times, sl st in first ch. Pull tail of center ring to close loop.

Round 2: ch 1, (sc 1, ch 3, pc, ch 6, sl st into first ch, ch 7, sl st into same stitch, ch 5, sl st into top of pc, ch 3) six times. Sl st in first ch to finish row.

Cut yarn, leaving a 6-in. tail, and pull through. Weave in ends to finish.

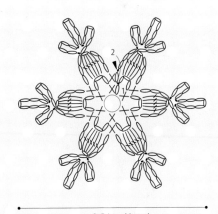

2.5 ins. (6 cm)

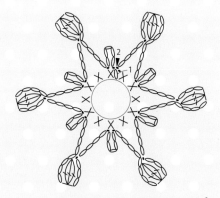

2.25 ins. (5.5 cm)

Snowflake C (bottom right in photo):

Note: Refer to the chart to see where on the previous round your stitches for the next round should be placed.

Using the crochet-in-the-round method, make a center ring.

Round 1: ch 1, sc 12, sl st in first ch. Pull tail of center ring to close loop.

Round 2: sl st in first sc from previous row, (ch 5, sl st in same st, ch 8, dc CL in fourth chain from hook, ch 3, sl st in same chain, ch 4, sl st in third sc of previous row) six times. Sl st in first ch to finish row.

Cut yarn, leaving a 6-in. tail, and pull through. Weave in ends to finish.

Holly Jolly Wreath

Materials:

- Medium-weight yarn (acrylic and wool blend) in brown, 15 yds (5g)
- Medium-weight yarn (acrylic and wool blend) in red and green 3 yds (1g) each

Tools:

- US size E/4 (3.5 mm) crochet hook
- Tapestry or yarn needle

Stitches Used:

Crochet: chain stitch (ch), single crochet (sc), single crochet decrease (sc2tog) and slip stitch (sl st). Piecing: whipstitch (see pages 10–13 for detailed instructions).

Wreath (make two):

Using brown yarn, begin with ch 46.

Row 1: Beginning in second chain from hook, sc 45, ch 1.

Row 2: sc 45. Cut yarn leaving a long tail and pull through.

Holly Berries (make three):

Using red yarn and the crochet-in-the-round method (see page 14 for detailed stitch instructions), make a center ring.

Round 1: ch 1, sc 6, sl st in first ch. Pull tail of center ring to close loop.

Round 2: ch 1, sc 6, sl st.

Round 3: ch 1, (sc2tog) three times, sl st.

Cut yarn, leaving a 6-in. tail, and pull through.

Holly Leaves (make two):

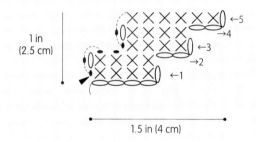

1 in (2.5 cm)

1.5 in (4 cm)

Using green yarn, begin with ch 5.

Row 1: Beginning in second chain from hook, sc 4, ch 1.

Row 2: sc 4, ch 3.

Row 3: Beginning in second chain from hook, sc 4, ch 1.

Row 4: sc 4, ch 3.

Row 5: Beginning in second chain from hook, sc 6.

Using the chart for reference, sl st 6 around the edge back to beginning.

Cut yarn, leaving a 6-in. tail, and pull through.

Sew the Pieces Together:

Fold a long wreath piece in half lengthwise, and use the whipstitch to stitch closed. Repeat on the second wreath piece. Twist the two pieces together and stitch ends together to form a ring. Stitch the two leaves together and then sew the berries to the leaves. Place the holly leaves and berries over the seam where the wreath ends meet and stitch in place to finish.

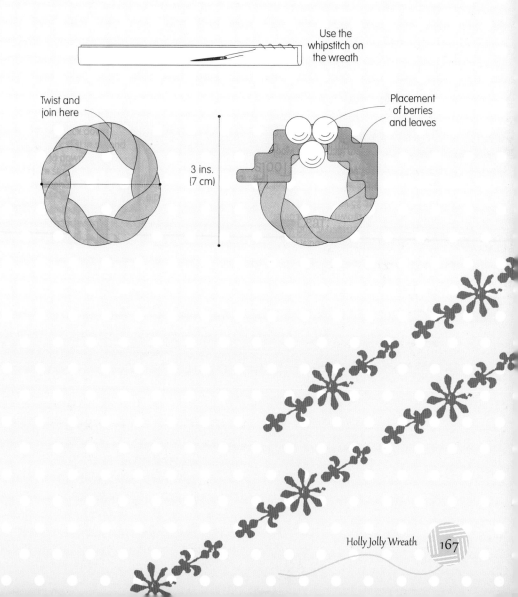

Use the whipstitch on the wreath

Twist and join here

3 ins. (7 cm)

Placement of berries and leaves

Gift Boxes

Materials:

- Medium-weight yarn (acrylic and wool blend) in color of your choice, 16 yds (7g)
- Ribbon or colorful yarn, 20 ins. per box

Tools:

- US size D/3 (3 mm) crochet hook
- Tapestry or yarn needle
- Kitchen sponge or craft foam, 1.5 ins. (3.5 cm) square

Stitches Used:

Crochet: chain stitch (ch), single crochet (sc,) slip stitch (sl st) and through the back loop (tbl). Piecing: whipstitch. (See pages 10–13 for detailed stitch instructions.)

Gift Box, Side A:

Begin with ch 8.

Row 1: Beginning with second ch from hook, sc 7, ch 1.

Note: Work all sts of rows 9, 17 and 25 tbl.

Rows 2–32: sc 7, ch 1. At the end of row 32, cut yarn, leaving an 8-in. tail, and pull through.

Gift Box, Side B (make two):

Begin with ch 8.

Row 1: Beginning with second ch from hook, sc 7, ch 1.

Rows 2–8: sc 7, ch 1. At the end of row 32, cut yarn, leaving an 8-in. tail, and pull through.

Sew the Pieces Together:

Using the whipstitch, sew row 1 and row 32 together on side A. Line up side B with the corners to the rows worked through the back loop. Use the whipstitch to attach. Insert sponge or foam block, and sew up second side, lining up the corners the same way. Weave in any ends. Tie ribbon around box with a bow to finish.

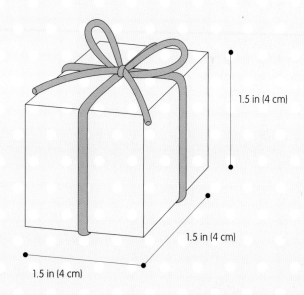

1.5 in (4 cm)

1.5 in (4 cm)

1.5 in (4 cm)

O Tannenbaum!

Materials:

Large Fir Tree

- Medium-weight yarn (acrylic and wool blend) in dark green, 38 yds (16g)

Medium Fir Tree

- Medium-weight yarn (acrylic and wool blend) in dark green, 20 yds (8g) each

- Medium-weight yarn (acrylic and wool blend) in light green, 8 yds (3g) each

Small Fir Tree

- Medium-weight yarn (acrylic and wool blend) in light green, 20 yds (8g) each

Christmas Tree

- Medium-weight yarn (acrylic and wool blend) in bright green, 25 yds (11g)

- 21 small pearl seed beads for ornaments

For All Trees

- Medium-weight yarn (acrylic and wool blend) in brown, 10 yds (4g) each

Tools:
- US size E/4 (3.5 mm) and G/6 (4 mm) crochet hooks
- Tapestry or yarn needle
- Toy stuffing, small amount
- Locking stitch marker

Stitches Used:
Crochet: chain stitch (ch), double crochet (dc), double crochet increase (dc inc), single crochet (sc), single crochet increase (sc inc) slip stitch (sl st) and through the back loop (tbl). (See pages 10–13 for detailed crochet stitch instructions.)

Use One Basic Pattern:

For small fir tree: use one size A tree bough and one size B tree bough.

For medium fir tree: two size A boughs in different shades of green, and one size B bough.

For large fir tree: use two size A boughs and two size B boughs.

For Christmas tree: two size A boughs and one size B bough.

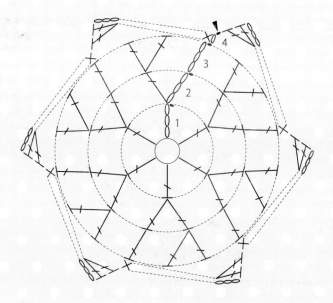

Tree Boughs, Size A:
Use the G/6 crochet hook and your choice of tree color yarn. Begin with the crochet-in-the-round method (see detailed instructions on page 16) and make a center ring.

Round 1: ch 3, dc 5, sl st. Pull tail to close center ring.

Round 2: ch 3, dc into same stitch as turning chain, (dc inc) five times, sl st.

Round 3: ch 3, (dc inc, dc 1) five times, dc inc, sl st.

Round 4: ch 1, (sc 1, ch 3, dc 2) in first stitch. (Skip two stitches, sc 1, ch 3, dc 2) six times, sl st. Cut yarn, leaving a long tail, and pull through.

Tree Boughs, Size B:

Use the G/6 crochet hook and your choice of tree color yarn. Begin with the crochet-in-the-round method and make a center ring.

Round 1: ch 3, dc 7, sl st. Pull tail to close center ring.

Round 2: ch 3, dc into same stitch as turning chain, (dc inc) seven times, sl st.

Round 3: ch 3, (dc inc, dc 1) seven times, dc inc, sl st.

Round 4: ch 1, (sc 1, ch 3, dc 2) in first stitch. (Skip two stitches, sc 1, ch 3, dc 2) eight times, sl st. Cut yarn, leaving a long tail, and pull through.

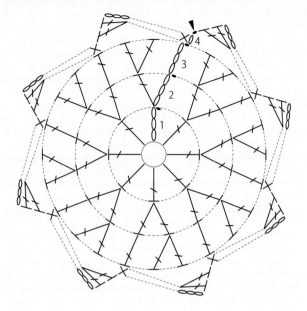

Tree Trunk (for all trees):

Use the E/4 crochet hook and brown yarn. Begin with the crochet-in-the-round method and make a center ring.

Round 1: ch 1, sc 7, sl st.

Round 2: ch 1, (sc inc) seven times, sl st.

Round 3: *Note: Work all sts of this round tbl.* Ch 1, sc 14, sl st.

Round 4: ch 1, sc 14, sl st.

Round 5: ch 1, (sc 5, sc2tog) twice, sl st.

Round 6: ch 1, sc 12, sl st.

Round 7: ch 1, sc 2, sc2tog, sc 4, sc2tog, sc 2, sl st.

Rounds 8–9: ch 1, sc 10, sl st.

Round 10: ch 1, (sc 3, sc2tog) twice, sl st.

Round 11: ch 1, sc 8, sl st.

Round 12: ch 1, (sc 2, sc2tog) twice, sl st. Cut yarn, leaving a long tail and pull through.

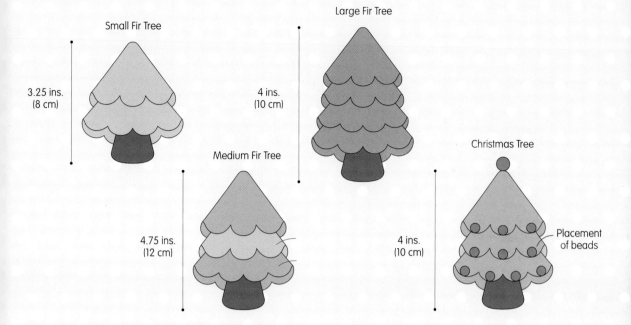

Small Fir Tree

3.25 ins.
(8 cm)

Large Fir Tree

4 ins.
(10 cm)

Medium Fir Tree

4.75 ins.
(12 cm)

Christmas Tree

4 ins.
(10 cm)

Placement
of beads

Sew the Pieces Together:

Stuff the tree trunk with toy stuffing. Weave the tail around the top row and pull tight to close. Stack the size A tree boughs on top on the size B boughs in all variations. Draw the yarn tail from the top size A boughs through the others, tie together to top of tree trunk and pull back through. For Christmas tree, sew beads to ends of each leaf, and to top of tree. Weave in any ends to finish.

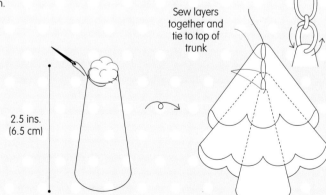

2.5 ins.
(6.5 cm)

Sew layers
together and
tie to top of
trunk

Abbreviations

Here is a quick guide to all the abbreviations that were used throughout this book.

( )	work instructions within parentheses as many times as directed
ch	chain stitch
cm	centimeter(s)
dc	double crochet
dc2tog	double crochet two stitches together
dc3tog	double crochet three stitches together
dc CL	double crochet cluster
dc CL inc	double crochet cluster increase
dc inc	double crochet increase
g	gram(s)
hdc	half-double crochet
in(s)	inches
inc	increase
mm	millimeters
p	picot stitch
pc	popcorn stitch
sc	single crochet
sc inc	single crochet increase
sc3inc	single crochet three stitches in one stitch
sc2tog	single crochet two stitches together
sc3tog	single crochet three stitches together
sl st	slip stitch
st(s)	stitches
tch	turning chain
tbl	through the back loop
tr	triple crochet
v-st	v-stitch
yd(s)	yards

About the Author

Maki Oomaci is a fiber artist and a tea ceremony instructor in Japan. She is the author of several Japanese books on food and crafts.